The
Quotable
George W. Bush

The
Quotable
George W. Bush

A PORTRAIT
IN HIS OWN WORDS

BILL ADLER

Andrews McMeel
Publishing

Kansas City

04 05 06 07 08 KP1 10 9 8 7 6 5 4 3 2 1

ISBN: 0-7407-4154-3

Library of Congress Control Number: 2003113254

Contents

CONTENTS

Introduction

OUR FORTY-THIRD PRESIDENT

When George Walker Bush was born on July 6, 1946, to George Herbert Walker Bush and Barbara Pierce Bush in New Haven, Connecticut, politics were already pumping in his blood. His grandfather, Prescott Bush, was a senator from Connecticut, and his mother was related to President Franklin Pierce. He was the first son in a family that eventually included two sisters and three brothers; his sister Robin died of leukemia in October 1953. She was not quite four years old.

By then the Bushes had already relocated from Connecticut to Midland, Texas. There, George W. grew up, watching his father making quite a go of the booming oil business in the 1950s and later entering the world of politics in the 1960s.

He followed his father's footsteps by attending the preparatory school Andover and, later, Yale University. After graduating with a degree in history from Yale in 1968, he served as an F-102 fighter pilot in the National Guard reserves. Eventually he returned to school to earn an MBA from the Harvard Business School, then he returned to Midland, Texas, where he set up a new oil company. It was during this period that he met a librarian named Laura Welch, whom he married in November 1977. In 1981, Laura gave birth to their twin daughters, Barbara and Jenna, named after their grandmothers.

After he helped lead his father's successful presidential campaign in 1988, George W. gathered a group of investors who purchased the Texas Rangers in 1989. He served as managing general partner of the Texas Rangers until he became governor of Texas on November 8, 1994, beating the immensely popular incumbent, Governor Ann Richards; he was reelected four years later.

When Governor Bush decided to run for the presidency, he had of course no idea that he would become most famous for the highly controversial presidential election of 2000, during which the state of Florida—where his brother Jeb was governor—became the center of doubt as to the number of votes that were cast and properly counted. Things got so out of control that the Republicans forced the Supreme Court to decide who was the president.

Regardless of the laws passed by his administration, it appears that President George W. Bush will always be most remembered as the president who led the country after the September 11 attacks on both the World Trade Center in New York City and the Pentagon just outside Washington, D.C. He declared war on terrorism, and proclaimed that the Iraqi dictator, Saddam Hussein, was planning to use weapons of mass destruction.

INTRODUCTION

The media have always found each president fascinating in his own right, but with President George W. Bush, they quickly discovered that he was not at all shy about expressing his opinions and that his quotes reflected his decisive leadership style. More than that, such strong leadership was needed in times of great uncertainty. Here, through all his State of the Union addresses and speeches to the world, he has made himself an eloquent political speaker. Until he writes his next autobiography, presumably after he leaves the White House, this book is the closest thing we have to a living political autobiography of the most important years of George W. Bush's life.

The
Quotable
George W. Bush

On Leadership and
the Presidency

"Presidents, whether things are good or bad, get the blame.
I understand that."

—Press conference, Washington, D.C., May 11, 2001

"[Winston Churchill] knew what he believed, and he really
kind of went after it in a way that seemed like a Texan to me. . . .
Sometimes Churchill will talk back, sometimes he won't,
depending upon the stress of the moment, but he is a constant
reminder of what a great leader is like."

—After receiving a bust of Churchill
from British Prime Minister Tony Blair,
Washington, D.C., July 16, 2001

"If you're one of these types of people that are always trying to
figure out which way the wind is blowing, decision making can
be difficult. But I find that I know who I am. I know what I believe

in, and I know where I want to lead the country. And most of the time, decisions come pretty easily for me, to be frank with you. I realize sometimes people don't like the decisions. That's okay. I've never been one to try to please everybody all the time. I just do what I think is right."

—*ATLANTIC UNBOUND*, FEBRUARY 12, 2003

"It's an interesting question about leadership. Does a leader lead, or does a leader follow? Does a leader lead opinion, or does a leader try to chase public opinion? My view is the leader leads. . . . I understand a leader can't do everything. And so, therefore, a leader must be willing to surround himself, in my case, with smart, capable, honorable people. A leader must be willing to listen. And then a leader must be decisive enough to make a decision and stick by it. In politics, in order to lead, you've got to know what you believe. You have to stand on principle, you have to believe in certain values. And you must defend them at all costs. A politician who takes a poll to figure out what to believe is a politician who is . . . like a dog chasing its tail. And, finally, any leader must . . . have a vision about where you're going."

—AT A DISCUSSION ABOUT LEADERSHIP AT
ST. PETERSBURG UNIVERSITY IN
ST. PETERSBURG, RUSSIA, MAY 25, 2002

"I think anybody who doesn't think I'm smart enough to handle the job is underestimating."

—*U.S. NEWS & WORLD REPORT*, APRIL 3, 2000

"No one is going to threaten the governor of the state of Texas. . . . My job is to enforce the laws of the state of Texas. That is my job and that is what I intend to do."

—IN RESPONSE TO CALLS BY THE CANADIAN GOVERNMENT,
USA TODAY, AMNESTY INTERNATIONAL, AND
U.S. SECRETARY OF STATE MADELEINE ALBRIGHT
TO GRANT A STAY OF EXECUTION FOR DEATH ROW INMATE
STAN FAULDER, SAN ANTONIO, TEXAS, DECEMBER 1998

"I can hear a guy breathing quite heavily. 'Mr. President! Mr. President! There's an unidentified aircraft heading toward the White House.' So we get out of bed. I'm actually in my running shorts with a T-shirt, old shoes."

—*NEWSWEEK*, NOVEMBER 26, 2001

On Campaigning

"I understand I'm running against a person who is so anxious to become president, he will do whatever it takes."

—On Al Gore,
the 2000 Democratic
presidential candidate

He was very frustrated with how his opponent Kent Hance made fun of him while campaigning in West Texas in his early days as a politician. "Would you like me to run as Sam Smith? The problem is, I can't abandon my background."

—First Son by Bill Minutaglio

"It is incredibly presumptive for somebody who has not yet earned his party's nomination to start speculating about vice presidents."

—Keene, New Hampshire, October 22, 1999,
as reported by the New Republic,
November 15, 1999

"Frankly, getting whipped was probably a pretty good thing for me."

— ON HIS FIRST DEFEAT IN HIS CONGRESSIONAL RACE,
AS REPORTED IN *FIRST SON* BY BILL MINUTAGLIO

"And I'm here to campaign for John Kline for the United States House of Representatives. If the good folks in his district are wise, they'll send him to Washington."

— COLEMAN, KLINE/MINNESOTA
REPUBLICAN PARTY VICTORY 2002 DINNER,
MINNEAPOLIS, MINNESOTA, JULY 11, 2002

"If you're happy with the status quo, don't vote for me."

— HIS SLOGAN WHILE RUNNING FOR
THE GOVERNORSHIP OF TEXAS

"After all, he [Al Gore] claimed he invented the Internet. But if he's so smart, how come every Internet address begins with 'W'?"

— NOVEMBER 4, 2000

"I didn't—I swear I didn't—get into politics to feather my nest or feather my friends' nests."

— *HOUSTON CHRONICLE*

"I've got a reason for running. I talk about a larger goal, which is to call upon the best of America. It's part of the renewal. It's reform and renewal. Part of the renewal is a set of high standards and to remind people that the greatness of America really does depend on neighbors helping neighbors and children finding mentors. I worry. I'm very worried about, you know, the kid who just wonders whether America is meant for him. I really worry about that . . . so, I'm running for a reason . . . you cannot lead America to a positive tomorrow with revenge on one's mind. Revenge is so incredibly negative. And so to answer your question, I'm going to win because people sense my heart, know my sense of optimism and know where I want to lead the country. . . . I'm an optimistic person. I'm an inherently content person. I've got a great sense of where I want to lead and I'm comfortable with why I'm running. And, you know, the call on that speech was, beware. This is going to be a tough campaign."

—*WASHINGTON POST*, MARCH 23, 2000

"I don't want to win? If that were the case, why the heck am I on the bus sixteen hours a day, shaking thousands of hands, giving hundreds of speeches, getting pillared in the press and cartoons and still staying on message to win?"

—*NEWSWEEK*, FEBRUARY 28, 2000

"Really proud of it. A great campaign. And I'm really pleased with the organization and the thousands of South Carolinians that worked on my behalf."

—TO THE REPORTER COKIE ROBERTS ON
THE TV PROGRAM *THIS WEEK*, FEBRUARY 20, 2000

"If you're sick and tired of the politics of cynicism and polls and principles, come and join this campaign."

—HILTON HEAD, SOUTH CAROLINA, FEBRUARY 16, 2000

"Thank you for your e-mail. This Internet of yours is a wonderful invention."

—FROM AN E-MAIL TO AL GORE,
AS REPORTED BY *NEWSWEEK*, MARCH 2000

"The administration I'll bring is a group of men and women who are focused on what's best for America—honest men and women, decent men and women, women who will see service to our country as a great privilege and who will not stain the house."

— FROM A *DES MOINES REGISTER* DEBATE,
DES MOINES, IOWA, JANUARY 15, 2000

"The important question is, how many hands have I shaked?"

— WHEN ASKED WHY HE HADN'T SPENT MORE TIME
CAMPAIGNING IN NEW HAMPSHIRE,
NEW YORK TIMES, OCTOBER 23, 1999

"Baseball is a pursuit for optimists, just like drilling for oil or running for office. To come to the ballpark every day, you have to believe you can win. To drill another well after a dry hole, you have to believe this one will be successful. To run for office, especially after losing, you have to believe you can win."

— *A CHARGE TO KEEP* BY GEORGE W. BUSH

"I've been consistent throughout the course of the campaign that my Supreme Court will be people that will not use the bench from which to legislate."

— *USA TODAY*, NOVEMBER 3, 2000

"I know something about being a governor, and I know what it takes to get elected."

— MANCHESTER, NEW HAMPSHIRE, OCTOBER 5, 2002

"I don't make any apologies for what I do on the campaign trail."

— *NEW YORK TIMES*, FEBRUARY 24, 2000

"This is what I'm good at. I like meeting people, my fellow citizens; I like interfacing with them."
— OUTSIDE PITTSBURGH, PENNSYLVANIA,
SEPTEMBER 8, 2000

"There's a huge trust. I see it all the time when people come up to me and say, 'I don't want you to let me down again.'"
— BOSTON, MASSACHUSETTS, OCTOBER 3, 2000

"I don't know whether I'm going to win or not. I think I am. I do know I'm ready for the job."
— DES MOINES, IOWA, AUGUST 21, 2000

His Inaugural Address

JANUARY 20, 2001

President Clinton, distinguished guests, and my fellow citizens, the peaceful transfer of authority is rare in history, yet common in our country. With a simple oath, we affirm old traditions and make new beginnings.

As I begin, I thank President Clinton for his service to our nation.

And I thank Vice President Gore for a contest conducted with spirit and ended with grace.

I am honored and humbled to stand here, where so many of America's leaders have come before me, and so many will follow.

We have a place, all of us, in a long story—a story we continue, but whose end we will not see. It is the story of a new world that became a friend and liberator of the old, a story of a slave-holding society that became a servant of freedom, the story of a power that went into the world to protect but not possess, to defend but not to conquer.

It is the American story—a story of flawed and fallible people, united across the generations by grand and enduring ideals.

The grandest of these ideals is an unfolding American promise that everyone belongs, that everyone deserves a chance, that no insignificant person was ever born.

Americans are called to enact this promise in our lives and in our laws. And though our nation has sometimes halted, and sometimes delayed, we must follow no other course.

Through much of the last century, America's faith in freedom and democracy was a rock in a raging sea. Now it is a seed upon the wind, taking root in many nations.

Our democratic faith is more than the creed of our country, it is the inborn hope of our humanity, an ideal we carry but do not own, a trust we bear and pass along. And even after nearly 225 years, we have a long way yet to travel.

While many of our citizens prosper, others doubt the promise, even the justice, of our own country. The ambitions of some Americans are limited by failing schools and hidden prejudice and the circumstances of their birth. And sometimes our differences run so deep, it seems we share a continent, but not a country.

We do not accept this, and we will not allow it. Our unity, our union, is the serious work of leaders and citizens in every generation. And this is my solemn pledge: I will work to build a single nation of justice and opportunity.

I know this is in our reach because we are guided by a power larger than ourselves who creates us equal in His image.

And we are confident in principles that unite and lead us onward.

America has never been united by blood or birth or soil. We are bound by ideals that move us beyond our backgrounds, lift us above our interests, and teach us what it means to be citizens. Every child must be taught these principles. Every citizen must uphold them. And every immigrant, by embracing these ideals, makes our country more, not less, American.

Today, we affirm a new commitment to live out our nation's promise through civility, courage, compassion, and character.

America, at its best, matches a commitment to principle with a concern for civility. A civil society demands from each of us goodwill and respect, fair dealing and forgiveness.

Some seem to believe that our politics can afford to be petty because, in a time of peace, the stakes of our debates appear small.

But the stakes for America are never small. If our country does not lead the cause of freedom, it will not be led. If we do not turn the hearts of children toward knowledge and character, we will lose their gifts and undermine their idealism. If we permit our economy to drift and decline, the vulnerable will suffer most.

We must live up to the calling we share. Civility is not a tactic or a sentiment. It is the determined choice of trust over cynicism, of community over chaos. And this commitment, if we keep it, is a way to shared accomplishment.

America, at its best, is also courageous.

Our national courage has been clear in times of depression and war, when defending common dangers defined our common good. Now we must choose if the example of our fathers and mothers will inspire us or condemn us. We must show courage in a time of blessing by confronting problems instead of passing them on to future generations.

Together, we will reclaim America's schools, before ignorance and apathy claim more young lives.

We will reform Social Security and Medicare, sparing our children from struggles we have the power to prevent. And we will reduce taxes, to recover the momentum of our economy and reward the effort and enterprise of working Americans.

We will build our defenses beyond challenge, lest weakness invite challenge.

We will confront weapons of mass destruction, so that a new century is spared new horrors.

The enemies of liberty and our country should make no mistake: America remains engaged in the world by history and by choice, shaping a balance of power that favors freedom. We will defend our allies and our interests. We will show purpose without arrogance. We will meet aggression and bad faith with resolve and strength. And to all nations, we will speak for the values that gave our nation birth.

America, at its best, is compassionate. In the quiet of American conscience, we know that deep, persistent poverty is unworthy of our nation's promise.

And whatever our views of its cause, we can agree that children at risk are not at fault. Abandonment and abuse are not acts of God, they are failures of love.

And the proliferation of prisons, however necessary, is no substitute for hope and order in our souls.

Where there is suffering, there is duty. Americans in need are not strangers, they are citizens, not problems, but priorities. And all of us are diminished when any are hopeless.

Government has great responsibilities for public safety and public health, for civil rights and common schools. Yet compassion is the work of a nation, not just a government.

And some needs and hurts are so deep they will only respond to a mentor's touch or a pastor's prayer. Church and charity, synagogue and mosque lend our communities their humanity, and they will have an honored place in our plans and in our laws.

Many in our country do not know the pain of poverty, but we can listen to those who do.

And I can pledge our nation to a goal: When we see that wounded traveler on the road to Jericho, we will not pass to the other side.

America, at its best, is a place where personal responsibility is valued and expected.

Encouraging responsibility is not a search for scapegoats, it is a call to conscience. And though it requires sacrifice, it brings a deeper fulfillment. We find the fullness of life not only in options, but in commitments. And we find that children and community are the commitments that set us free.

Our public interest depends on private character, on civic duty and family bonds and basic fairness, on uncounted, un-honored acts of decency which give direction to our freedom.

Sometimes in life we are called to do great things. But as a saint of our times has said, every day we are called to do small things with great love. The most important tasks of a democracy are done by everyone.

I will live and lead by these principles: to advance my con-victions with civility, to pursue the public interest with courage, to speak for greater justice and compassion, to call for responsi-bility and try to live it as well.

In all these ways, I will bring the values of our history to the care of our times.

What you do is as important as anything government does. I ask you to seek a common good beyond your comfort; to defend needed reforms against easy attacks; to serve your nation, beginning with your neighbor. I ask you to be citizens: citizens, not spectators; citizens, not subjects; responsible citizens, building communities of service and a nation of character.

Americans are generous and strong and decent, not because we believe in ourselves, but because we hold beliefs beyond ourselves. When this spirit of citizenship is missing, no government program can replace it. When this spirit is present, no wrong can stand against it.

After the Declaration of Independence was signed, Virginia statesman John Page wrote to Thomas Jefferson: "We know the race is not to the swift nor the battle to the strong. Do you not think an angel rides in the whirlwind and directs this storm?"

Much time has passed since Jefferson arrived for his inauguration. The years and changes accumulate. But the themes of this day he would know: our nation's grand story of courage and its simple dream of dignity.

We are not this story's author, who fills time and eternity with his purpose. Yet his purpose is achieved in our duty, and our duty is fulfilled in service to one another.

Never tiring, never yielding, never finishing, we renew that purpose today, to make our country more just and generous, to affirm the dignity of our lives and every life.

This work continues. This story goes on. And an angel still rides in the whirlwind and directs this storm.

God bless you all, and God bless America.

On the Environment

"Listen, we've got a lot of work to do to make sure the Forest Service has got wise forest policy—to make sure to maintain the forests so that they're healthy and viable, and not become kindling boxes."

—Eagar, Arizona, June 25, 2002

"It's a meaningful piece of legislation for this part of the country because a lot of people make their living on the farm and on the ranch. And we want our families to be on the farms and ranch."

—On signing the 2001 Farm Bill, August 13, 2001

"Imagine how less dependent America will be on foreign sources of energy, and how . . . easy it'll be to clean up our air."

—On the development of fuel cell technology, Washington, D.C., February 25, 2002

"We also need to conserve more, and conservation comes as a result of new technologies."

—From an interview with John King
on CNN, April 25, 2001

"We need to thin. We need to make our forests healthy by using some common sense. . . . We need to understand, if you let kindling build up and there's a lightning strike, you're going to get yourself a big fire."

—Unveiling his "Healthy Forests" plan,
Central Point, Oregon, August 22, 2002

"One of these days, this little lady right here is going to be driving an automobile with a hybrid engine in it, and a fuel cell in it. And it's going to work. And I hope I'm around to see it, too."

—Washington, D.C., February 25, 2002

"[All] land is precious, but the part that the people uniformly would not want to spoil, will not be despoiled. . . . There are parts of the monument lands where we can explore without affecting the overall environment."

—On the oil-drilling potential of
national monuments at a media round table,
Washington, D.C., March 13, 2001

"It doesn't make any sense to have a forest policy that will not allow for thinning and clearing, a forest policy that is so backward that we allow kindling to build up in these forests, and then with an act of nature, or with a sleight of hand by mankind, our national treasures burn to the ground."

—Northern State University, Aberdeen,
South Dakota, October 31, 2002

"People are beginning to get the message. I mean, Americans who have no idea what good forest policy means are beginning to see the fires on TV. It's a sad way for people to learn, but it's happening, and we're beginning to make some progress."

—Unveiling his "Healthy Forests" plan,
Central Point, Oregon, August 22, 2002

On Business and the Economy

"It's an encroachment on the executive branch's ability to conduct business."

—Response to investigators asking for the names of
Enron executives who'd met with him
in energy policy meetings, January 28, 2002

"Let me tell you, Bobby, how you do quantitative analysis. You do all your analysis, you do all your statistics, and then you punch a hole in the ground. And if there's no oil there, you just lost five million bucks."

—Explaining to one of his friends how the oil game in Texas
was played, as reported in First Son by Bill Minutaglio

"But corporate America has got to understand there's a higher calling than trying to fudge the numbers, trying to slip a billion here or a billion there and hope nobody notices."

—Washington, D.C., June 28, 2002

"A job is the best thing that you can [give] to help anybody."
—FROM REMARKS TO MARTHA'S TABLE VOLUNTEERS AND
BOARD OF DIRECTORS, WASHINGTON, D.C., DECEMBER 20, 2001

"Derek is the CEO of a small bio-tech firm. . . . He started what's called 'St. Louis Cares.' It is a recruiting vehicle to help match people with kind hearts with people who need kind hearts in their lives. And the reason I want to talk about the Dereks of the world is because in order to win the war against evil, this nation must continue to practice acts of decency and kindness and goodness. That there is no question that the entrepreneurial spirit in America makes us unique."
—ALBERS MANUFACTURING, O'FALLON, MISSOURI,
MARCH 18, 2002

"We've got to be able to put the right people in the right job at the right time, without a thick book of rules that have little to do with protecting the American people."
—MADISON CENTRAL HIGH SCHOOL,
MADISON, MISSISSIPPI, AUGUST 7, 2002

"I believe people have taken a step back and asked, 'What's important in life?' You know, the bottom line and this corporate America stuff, is that important? Or is serving your neighbor, loving your neighbor like you'd like to be loved yourself?"
—MINNEAPOLIS, MINNESOTA, JULY 11, 2002

"Ann and I will carry out this equivocal message to the world: Markets must be open."
—AT SECRETARY OF AGRICULTURE
ANN VENEMAN'S SWEARING-IN CEREMONY,
WASHINGTON, D.C., MARCH 2, 2001

"I want to congratulate you all for achieving an . . . historic moment in our nation, because what you all have done is you've made it much more likely somebody is going to be able to find work, and some farmer is going to be able to sell his product, and some nation is going to be able to trade with us, which will help lift them out of poverty."

—COMMENDING BIPARTISAN LEADERS ON TRADE AGREEMENT, WASHINGTON, D.C., AUGUST 1, 2002

"I think work is incredibly important. Work leads to dignity."

—STOCKTON, CALIFORNIA, AUGUST 23, 2002

"But I do want to thank you for your hospitality and all the employees with whom I just had an interesting discussion . . . about what's on their mind, about what's it like to work for a small business and . . . what the government can do to perhaps make the small business more vibrant and/or deal with some of the needs that directly affect the employees."

—ALBERS MANUFACTURING, O'FALLON, MISSOURI, MARCH 18, 2002

"Let me tell you my thoughts about tax relief. When your economy is kind of ooching along, it's important to let people have more of their own money."

—BOSTON, MASSACHUSETTS, OCTOBER 4, 2002

"I also understand how tender the free enterprise system can be."

—PRESS CONFERENCE, WASHINGTON, D.C., JULY 9, 2002

His First State of
the Union Address

FEBRUARY 27, 2001

Mr. Speaker, Mr. Vice President, members of Congress: It's a great privilege to be here to outline a new budget and a new approach for governing our great country. I thank you for your invitation to speak here tonight. I know Congress had to formally invite me, and it could have been a close vote. So, Mr. Vice President, I appreciate you being here to break the tie.

I want to thank so many of you who have accepted my invitation to come to the White House to discuss important issues. We're off to a good start. I will continue to meet with you and ask for your input. You have been kind and candid, and I thank you for making a new president feel welcome.

The last time I visited the Capitol, I came to take an oath on the steps of this building. I pledged to honor our Constitution and laws. And I asked you to join me in setting a tone of civility and respect in Washington.

I hope America is noticing the difference, because we're making progress. Together, we are changing the tone in the nation's capital. And this spirit of respect and cooperation is vital, because, in the end, we will be judged not only by what we say or how we say it, we will be judged by what we're able to accomplish.

America today is a nation with great challenges, but greater resources. An artist using statistics as a brush could paint two very different pictures of our country. One would have warning signs: increasing layoffs, rising energy prices, too many failing schools, persistent poverty, the stubborn vestiges of racism. Another picture would be full of blessings: a balanced budget, big surpluses, a military that is second to none, a country at peace with its neighbors, technology that is revolutionizing the world, and our greatest strength—concerned citizens who care for our country and care for each other.

Neither picture is complete in and of itself. And tonight I challenge and invite Congress to work with me to use the resources of one picture to repaint the other, to direct the advantages of our time to solve the problems of our people. Some of these resources will come from government. Some, but not all.

Year after year in Washington, budget debates seem to come down to an old, tired argument: on one side, those who want more government, regardless of the cost; on the other, those who want less government, regardless of the need. We should leave those arguments to the last century, and chart a different course.

Government has a role, and an important role. Yet, too much government crowds out initiative and hard work, private charity, and the private economy. Our new governing vision says government should be active, but limited; engaged, but not overbearing. And my budget is based on that philosophy.

It is reasonable, and it is responsible. It meets our obligations and funds our growing needs. We increase spending next year for Social Security and Medicare, and other entitlement programs, by $81 billion. We've increased spending for discretionary programs by a very responsible 4 percent, above the rate of inflation. My plan pays down an unprecedented amount of our national debt. And then, when money is still left over, my plan returns it to the people who earned it in the first place.

A budget's impact is counted in dollars but measured in lives. Excellent schools, quality health care, a secure retirement, a cleaner environment, a stronger defense—these are all important needs, and we fund them. The highest percentage increase in our budget should go to our children's education. Education is my top priority and, by supporting this budget, you'll make it yours, as well.

Reading is the foundation of all learning. So during the next five years, we triple spending, adding $5 billion to help every child in America learn to read. Values are important, so we've tripled funding for character education to teach our children not only reading and writing, but right from wrong.

We've increased funding to train and recruit teachers, because we know a good education starts with a good teacher. And I have a wonderful partner in this effort. I like teachers so much, I married one. Laura has begun a new effort to recruit Americans to the profession that will shape our future—teaching. She will travel across America to promote sound teaching practices and early reading skills in our schools and in programs such as Head Start.

When it comes to our schools, dollars alone do not always make the difference. Funding is important, and so is reform. So we must tie funding to higher standards and accountability for results.

I believe in local control of schools. We should not, and we will not, run public schools from Washington, D.C. Yet when the federal government spends tax dollars, we must insist on results. Children should be tested on basic reading and math skills every year between grades three and eight. Measuring is the only way to know whether all our children are learning. And I want to know, because I refuse to leave any child behind in America.

Critics of testing contend it distracts from learning. They talk about teaching to the test. But let's put that logic to the test. If you test a child on basic math and reading skills, and you're teaching to the test, you're teaching math and reading. And that's the whole idea. As standards rise, local schools will need more flexibility to meet them. So we must streamline the dozens of federal education programs into five, and let states spend money in those categories as they see fit.

Schools will be given a reasonable chance to improve and the support to do so. Yet, if they don't, if they continue to fail, we must give parents and students different options—a better public school, a private school, tutoring, or a charter school. In the end, every child in a bad situation must be given a better choice because when it comes to our children, failure is simply not an option.

Another priority in my budget is to keep the vital promises of Medicare and Social Security, and together we will do so. To meet the health care needs of all America's seniors, we double the Medicare budget over the next ten years. My budget dedicates $238 billion to Medicare next year alone, enough to fund all current programs and to begin a new prescription drug benefit for low-income seniors. No senior in America should have to choose between buying food and buying prescriptions.

To make sure the retirement savings of America's seniors are not diverted in any other program, my budget protects all $2.6 trillion of the Social Security surplus for Social Security, and for Social Security alone.

My budget puts a priority on access to health care, without telling Americans what doctor they have to see or what coverage they must choose. Many working Americans do not have health care coverage, so we will help them buy their own insurance with refundable tax credits. And to provide quality care in low-income neighborhoods, over the next five years we will double the number of people served at community health care centers.

And we will address the concerns of those who have health coverage, yet worry their insurance company doesn't care and won't pay. Together this Congress and this president will find common ground to make sure doctors make medical decisions, and patients get the health care they deserve with a patients' bill of rights.

When it comes to their health, people want to get the medical care they need, not be forced to go to court because they didn't get it. We will ensure access to the courts for those with legitimate claims. But first, let's put in place a strong, independent review so we promote quality health care, not frivolous lawsuits.

My budget also increases funding for medical research, which gives hope to many who struggle with serious disease.

Our prayers tonight are with one of your own who is engaged in his own fight against cancer—a fine representative, and a good man, Congressman Joe Moakley. I can think of no more appropriate tribute to Joe than to have the Congress finish the job of doubling the budget for the National Institutes of Health.

My new Freedom Initiative for Americans with Disabilities funds new technologies, expands opportunities to work, and makes our society more welcoming. For the more than fifty million Americans with disabilities, we need to break down barriers to equality.

The budget I propose to you also supports the people who keep our country strong and free, the men and women who serve in the United States military. I'm requesting $5.7 billion in increased military pay and benefits, and health care and housing. Our men and women in uniform give America their best and we owe them our support.

America's veterans honored their commitment to our country through their military service. I will honor our commitment to them with a million-dollar increase to ensure better access to quality care and faster decisions on benefit claims.

My budget will improve our environment by accelerating the cleanup of toxic brownfields. And I propose we make a major investment in conservation by fully funding the Land and Water Conservation Fund. Our national parks have a special place in our country's life. Our parks are places of great natural beauty and history. As good stewards, we must leave them better than we found them. So I propose providing $4.9 billion over five years for the upkeep of these national treasures.

And my budget adopts a hopeful new approach to help the poor and the disadvantaged. We must encourage and support the work of charities and faith-based and community groups that offer help and love one person at a time. These groups are working in every neighborhood in America to fight homelessness and addiction and domestic violence; to provide a hot meal or a mentor or a safe haven for our children. Government should welcome these groups to apply for funds, not discriminate against them.

Government cannot be replaced by charities or volunteers. Government should not fund religious activities. But our nation should support the good works of these good people who are helping their neighbors in need. So I propose allowing all taxpayers, whether they itemize or not, to deduct their charitable contributions. Estimates show this could encourage as much as $14 billion a year in new charitable giving, money that will save and change lives.

Our budget provides more than $700 million over the next ten years for a federal compassion capital fund, with a focused and noble mission, to provide a mentor to the more than 100 million children with a parent in prison, and to support other local efforts to fight illiteracy, teen pregnancy, drug addiction, and other difficult problems.

With us tonight is the mayor of Philadelphia. Please help me welcome mayor John Street. Mayor Street has encouraged faith-based and community organizations to make a significant difference in Philadelphia. He's invited me to his city this summer to see compassionate action. I'm personally aware of just how effective the mayor is. Mayor Street's a Democrat. Let the record show, I lost his city, big time. But some things are bigger than politics. So I look forward to coming to your city, to see your faith-based programs in action.

As government promotes compassion, it also must promote justice. Too many of our citizens have cause to doubt our nation's justice, when the law points a finger of suspicion at groups, instead of individuals. All our citizens are created equal and must be treated equally.

Earlier today, I asked John Ashcroft, the attorney general, to develop specific recommendations to end racial profiling. It's wrong and we will end it in America. In so doing, we will not hinder the work of our nation's brave police officers. They protect us every day—often at great risk. But by stopping the abuses of a few, we will add to the public confidence our police officers earn and deserve.

My budget has funded a responsible increase in our ongoing operations. It has funded our nation's important priorities. It has protected Social Security and Medicare. And our surpluses are big enough that there is still money left over.

Many of you have talked about the need to pay down our national debt. I listened, and I agree. We owe it to our children and grandchildren to act now, and I hope you will join me to pay down $2 trillion in debt during the next ten years. At the end of those ten years, we will have paid down all the debt that is available to retire. That is more debt, repaid more quickly than has ever been repaid by any nation at any time in history.

We should also prepare for the unexpected, for the uncertainties of the future. We should approach our nation's budget as any prudent family would, with a contingency fund for emergencies or additional spending needs. For example, after a strategic review, we may need to increase defense spending. We may need to increase spending for our farmers or additional money to reform Medicare. And so, my budget sets aside almost a trillion dollars over ten years for additional needs. That is one trillion additional reasons you can feel comfortable supporting this budget.

We have increased our budget at a responsible 4 percent. We have funded our priorities. We paid down all the available debt. We have prepared for contingencies. And we still have money left over.

Yogi Berra once said, "When you come to a fork in the road, take it." Now, we come to a fork in the road; we have two choices. Even though we have already met our needs, we could spend the money on more and bigger government. That's the road our nation has traveled in recent years.

Last year, government spending shot up 8 percent. That's far more than our economy grew, far more than personal income grew, and far more than the rate of inflation. If you continue on that road, you will spend the surplus and have to dip into Social Security to pay other bills. Unrestrained government spending is a dangerous road to deficits, so we must take a different path. The other choice is to let the American people spend their own money to meet their own needs.

I hope you will join me in standing firmly on the side of the people. You see, the growing surplus exists because taxes are too high and government is charging more than it needs. The people of America have been overcharged and, on their behalf, I am here asking for a refund.

Some say my tax plan is too big. Others say it's too small. I respectfully disagree. This plan is just right. I didn't throw darts at the board to come up with a number for tax relief. I didn't take a poll or develop an arbitrary formula that might sound good. I looked at problems in the Tax Code and calculated the cost to fix them.

A tax rate of 15 percent is too high for those who earn low wages, so we must lower the rate to 10 percent. No one should pay more than a third of the money they earn in federal income taxes, so we lowered the top rate to 33 percent.

This reform will be welcome relief for America's small businesses, which often pay taxes at the highest rate. And help for small business means jobs for Americans. We simplified the Tax Code by reducing the number of tax rates from the current five rates to four lower ones, 10 percent, 15, 25, and 33 percent. In my plan, no one is targeted in or targeted out. Everyone who pays income taxes will get relief.

Our government should not tax, and thereby discourage, marriage, so we reduced the marriage penalty. I want to help families rear and support their children, so we doubled the child credit to $1,000 per child. It's not fair to tax the same earnings twice—once when you earn them, and again when you die—so we must repeal the death tax.

These changes add up to significant help. A typical family with two children will save $1,600 a year on their federal income taxes. Now, $1,600 may not sound like a lot to some, but it means a lot to many families: $1,600 buys gas for two cars for an entire year; it pays tuition for a year at a community college; it pays the average family grocery bill for three months. That's real money.

With us tonight representing many American families are Steven and Josefina Ramos. They are from Pennsylvania. But they could be from any one of your districts. Steven is the network administrator for a school district. Josefina is a Spanish teacher at a charter school. And they have a two-year-old daughter.

Steven and Josefina tell me they pay almost $8,000 a year in federal income taxes. My plan will save them more than $2,000. Let me tell you what Steven says: "Two thousand dollars a year means a lot to my family. If we had this money, it would help us reach our goal of paying off our personal debt in two years' time." After that, Steven and Josefina want to start saving for Lianna's college education.

My attitude is, government should never stand in the way of families, achieving their dreams. And as we debate this issue, always remember, the surplus is not the government's money, the surplus is the people's money.

For lower-income families, my tax plan restores basic fairness. Right now, complicated tax rules punish hard work. A waitress supporting two children on $25,000 a year can lose nearly half of every additional dollar she earns above the $25,000. Her overtime, her hardest hours, are taxed at nearly 20 percent. This sends a terrible message: You'll never get ahead. But America's message must be different. We must honor hard work, never punish it. With tax relief, overtime will no longer be over-taxed time for the waitress. People with the smallest incomes will get the highest percentage of reductions. And millions of additional American families will be removed from the income tax rolls entirely.

Tax relief is right and tax relief is urgent. The long economic expansion that began almost ten years ago is faltering. Lower interest rates will eventually help, but we cannot assume they will do the job all by themselves.

Forty years ago, and then twenty years ago, two presidents, one Democrat, one Republican, John F. Kennedy and Ronald Reagan, advocated tax cuts to, in President Kennedy's words, get this country moving again. They knew then what we must do now. To create economic growth and opportunity, we must put money back into the hands of the people who buy goods and create jobs.

We must act quickly. The chairman of the Federal Reserve has testified before Congress that tax cuts often come too late to stimulate economic recovery. So I want to work with you to give our economy an important jump-start by making tax relief retroactive.

We must act now because it is the right thing to do. We must also act now because we have other things to do. We must show courage to confront and resolve tough challenges, to restructure our nation's defenses, to meet our growing need for energy, and to reform Medicare and Social Security.

America has a window of opportunity to extend and secure our present peace by promoting a distinctly American internationalism. We will work with our allies and friends to be a force for good and a champion of freedom. We will work for free markets, free trade and freedom from oppression. Nations making progress toward freedom will find America is their friend. We will promote our values. We will promote the peace. And we need a strong military to keep the peace.

But our military was shaped to confront the challenges of the past. So I've asked the secretary of defense to review America's armed forces and prepare to transform them to meet emerging threats. My budget makes a down payment on the research and development that will be required. Yet, in our broader transformation effort, we must put strategy first, then spending. Our defense vision will drive our defense budget, not the other way around.

Our nation also needs a clear strategy to confront the threats of the 21st century—threats that are more widespread and less certain. They range from terrorists who threaten with bombs to tyrants in rogue nations intent upon developing weapons of mass destruction. To protect our own people, our allies and friends, we must develop and we must deploy effective missile defenses.

And as we transform our military, we can discard Cold War relics, and reduce our own nuclear forces to reflect today's needs. A strong America is the world's best hope for peace and freedom.

Yet the cause of freedom rests on more than our ability to defend ourselves and our allies. Freedom is exported every day, as we ship goods and products that improve the lives of millions of people. Free trade brings greater political and personal freedom. Each of the previous five presidents has had the ability to negotiate far-reaching trade agreements. Tonight I ask you to give me the strong hand of presidential trade promotion authority, and to do so quickly.

As we meet tonight, many citizens are struggling with the high cost of energy. We have a serious energy problem that demands a national energy policy. The West is confronting a major energy shortage that has resulted in high prices and uncertainty. I've asked federal agencies to work with California officials to help speed construction of new energy sources, and I have directed Vice President Cheney, Commerce Secretary Evans, Energy Secretary Abraham, and other senior members in my administration to develop a national energy policy.

Our energy demand outstrips our supply. We can produce more energy at home while protecting our environment, and we must. We can produce more electricity to meet demand, and we must. We can promote alternative energy sources and conservation, and we must. America must become more energy-independent, and we will.

Perhaps the biggest test of our foresight and courage will be reforming Medicare and Social Security. Medicare's finances are strained and its coverage is outdated. Ninety-nine percent of employer-provided health plans offer some form of prescription drug coverage; Medicare does not. The framework for reform has been developed by Senators Frist and Breaux and Congressman Thomas, and now is the time to act.

Medicare must be modernized, and we must make sure that every senior on Medicare can choose a health care plan that offers prescription drugs.

Seven years from now, the baby boom generation will begin to claim Social Security benefits. Every one in this chamber knows that Social Security is not prepared to fully fund their retirement. And we only have a couple of years to get prepared. Without reform, this country will one day awaken to a stark choice: either a drastic rise in payroll taxes or a radical cut in retirement benefits.

There is a better way. This spring I will form a presidential commission to reform Social Security. The commission will make its recommendations by next fall. Reform should be based on these principles: It must preserve the benefits of all current retirees and those nearing retirement. It must return Social Security to sound financial footing. And it must offer personal savings accounts to younger workers who want them.

Social Security now offers workers a return of less than 2 percent on the money they pay into the system. To save the system, we must increase that by allowing younger workers to make safe, sound investments that yield a higher rate of return. Ownership, access to wealth, and independence should not be the privilege of the few. They are the hope of every American, and we must make them the foundation of Social Security.

By confronting the tough challenge of reform, by being responsible with our budget, we can earn the trust of the American people. And we can add to that trust by enacting fair and balanced election and campaign reforms.

The agenda I have set before you tonight is worthy of a great nation. America is a nation at peace, but not a nation at rest. Much has been given to us, and much is expected. Let us agree to bridge old divides. But let us also agree that our goodwill must be dedicated to great goals. Bipartisan is more than minding our matters. It is doing our duty.

No one can speak in this Capitol and not be awed by its history. At so many turning points, debates in these chambers have reflected the collected or divided conscience of our country. And when we walk through Statuary Hall and see those men and women of marble, we're reminded of their courage and achievement.

Yet America's purpose is never found only in statues or history. America's purpose always stands before us. Our generation must show courage in a time of blessing, as our nation has always shown in times of crisis. And our courage, issue by issue, can gather to greatness and serve our country. This is the privilege and responsibility we share. And if we work together, we can prove that public service is noble.

We all came here for a reason. We all have things we want to accomplish and promises to keep. *Juntos podemos*—together we can.

We can make Americans proud of their government. Together we can share in the credit of making our country more prosperous and generous and just, and earn from our conscience and from our fellow citizens the highest possible praise: Well done, good and faithful servants.

Thank you all. Good night and God bless.

On Education

"It is time to set aside the old partisan bickering and finger-pointing and name-calling that comes from freeing parents to make different choices for their children."

— From remarks on "parental empowerment in education," Washington, D.C., April 12, 2001

"I was never a great intellectual. I like books and pick them up and read them for the fun of it. I think all of us [brothers and sister] are basically in the same vein. We're not real serious, studious readers. We are readers for fun."

— Dallas Morning News, February 23, 2003

"In order to go to college or realize your dreams, you have to make right choices in life. As you grow up, you've got to learn to say yes to the good things and no to the bad things, like saying no to drugs. That's going to be important in order to realize your dreams. No to alcohol, excessive alcohol. You've got to learn to make the right choices when you get older."

—Crawford Elementary School,
Crawford, Texas, August 23, 2001

"She's a fabulous, fabulous first lady—who is going to spend time reminding people that classroom teachers, people in the classroom, are incredibly important for America."

—Milwaukee, Wisconsin, May 8, 2002

"I want it to be said that the Bush administration was a results-oriented administration, because I believe the results of focusing our attention and energy on teaching children to read and having an education system that's responsive to the child and to the parents, as opposed to mired in a system that refuses to change, will make America what we want it to be—a literate country. . . ."

—Washington, D.C., January 11, 2001

"We must give our children a spirit of moral courage, because their character is our destiny. . . . Our schools must support the ideals of parents, elevating character and abstinence from afterthoughts to urgent goals."

—From his speech accepting the nomination of
the Republican Party for president of
the United States, August 3, 2000

"We must have the attitude that every child in America—regardless of where they're raised or how they're born—can learn."

—New Britain, Connecticut, April 18, 2001

"Making sure every child can read, making sure that we encourage faith-based organizations . . . when it comes to helping neighbors in need, making sure that our neighborhoods are safe, making sure that the State of Texas recognizes that people from all walks of life have got a shot at the Texas dream. . . ."

—When asked to define the phrase "compassionate conservatism" as the governor of Texas

"Reading is the new civil right. Because if you can't read, you cannot possibly be educated, and if you're not educated, you can't succeed. . . . We've got to make sure that everybody gets educated."

—Los Angeles, California, April 29, 2002

"In order for all Americans to realize the American Dream, you've got to make sure every child has the necessary foundation to be good reader, good writer, good comprehender."

—Pennsylvania State University, April 2, 2002

"To those of you who received honors, awards, and distinctions, I say well done. And to the C students, I say: You, too, can be president of the United States."

—Yale University, New Haven, Connecticut, 2001

On Money

"We've got to understand, in America there are pockets of despair and hopelessness, places where people hurt because they're not sure if America is meant for them, places where people are addicted. And government can help eradicate these pockets by handing out money. But what government cannot do is put hope in people's hearts and a sense of purpose in people's lives."

— Trenton, New Jersey, September 23, 2002

"You're going to hear the statisticians, the number crunchers, the bean counters—as we call them in Texas—say this might have been a recession. . . . Well, when they do that, they get crossways with the Bush boys."

— Republican Party of Florida reception,
St. Pete Beach, Florida, March 8, 2002

"We have conducted a thorough assessment of our military and reconstruction needs in Iraq, and also in Afghanistan. I will soon submit to Congress a request for $87 billion. The request will cover ongoing military and intelligence operations in Iraq, Afghanistan, and elsewhere, which we expect will cost $66 billion over the next year. This budget request will also support our commitment to helping the Iraqi and Afghan people rebuild their own nations, after decades of oppression and mismanagement. We will provide funds to help them improve security. And we will help them to restore basic services, such as electricity and water, and to build new schools, roads, and medical clinics. This effort is essential to the stability of those nations, and, therefore, to our own security. Now and in the future, we will support our troops and we will keep our word to the more than fifty million people of Afghanistan and Iraq."

—ADDRESS TO THE NATION, SEPTEMBER 7, 2003

"Anybody who goes into court and wins their case ought to get full economic damages. At the same time, we must prevent excessive awards that drive up costs, encourage frivolous lawsuits, and promote drawn-out legal proceedings. And that is why we need a reasonable federal limit on noneconomic damages awarded in medical liability lawsuits, and the reasonable limit in my judgment ought to be $250,000."

—GREENSBORO, NORTH CAROLINA, JULY 25, 2002

"You know, I remember campaigning in Chicago and somebody said, 'Would you ever spend a deficit?' And I said, only if we're at war or we had a recession or there was a national emergency. Little did I realize we'd get the trifecta."

—CHARLOTTE, NORTH CAROLINA, FEBRUARY 27, 2002

"I will do everything I can to defend . . . private property rights when I am the governor of this state."

— Repeatedly in speeches while campaigning
for the governorship of Texas

"I believe if you let a person keep their own money, that person is more likely to demand a good or a service. And when they demand a good or a service in our society, somebody is more likely to produce it."

— South Bend, Indiana, September 5, 2002

On Washington, D.C.

"I want to thank you for coming to the White House to give me an opportunity to urge you to work with these five senators and three congressmen, to work hard to get this trade promotion authority moving. The power that be—well, most of the power that be—sits right here."

—Washington, D.C., June 18, 2001

"[Bureaucrats are] always seeing the tunnel at the end of the light."

—Accepting the nomination of
the Republican Party for the presidency,
August 3, 2000

"But the truth of the matter is, we can't pass a law that says you'll love your neighbor like yourself. And we can't pass a law that says you will be honest. We can pass laws that say, if you're not honest, we'll get you."

—Birmingham, Alabama, July 15, 2002

"You know, in Washington there's . . . a lot of shrill voices, people . . . who like to divide people into camps and call names and point fingers."

—AT A CONGRESSIONAL CAMPAIGN LUNCHEON
IN ALBUQUERQUE, NEW MEXICO, APRIL 29, 2002

"There's no question that the minute I got elected, the storm clouds on the horizon were getting nearly directly overhead."

—WASHINGTON, D.C., MAY 11, 2001

"I think [Ambassador Zoellick] deserves a lot of credit. But don't give him any until he describes exactly what he did to you."

—FROM REMARKS MADE TO AGRICULTURE LEADERS
ON JUNE 18, 2001

"That's what politics is all about, as far as I'm concerned—it's the people's will."

—ABOARD *AIR FORCE ONE*, MARCH 9, 2001

"You know, sometimes in Washington we actually are able to put our political parties aside and focus on what's best for the country. And we're able to say, let's make sure America . . . is the first priority."

—WASHINGTON, D.C., MAY 14, 2002

"That's Washington. That's the place where you find people getting ready to jump out of the foxholes before the first shot is fired."

—WESTLAND, MICHIGAN, SEPTEMBER 8, 2000

"Paul Wellstone was a man of deep convictions, a plainspoken fellow who did his best for his state and for his country. May the good Lord bless those who grieve."

— ON THE DEATH OF DEMOCRATIC SENATOR
PAUL WELLSTONE OF MINNESOTA,
CRAWFORD, TEXAS, OCTOBER 25, 2002

"Great to have you back. Just don't steal the silverware."

— GREETING DEMOCRATIC NATIONAL COMMITTEE
CHAIRMAN TERRY McAULIFFE BEFORE
THE KENNEDY CENTER HONORS,
DECEMBER 2, 2001

"Government can hand out money and, frankly, we do a pretty good job of it sometimes."

— NEW ORLEANS, LOUISIANA, DECEMBER 3, 2002

"It's important for people to understand, particularly in Washington, this Department of Homeland Security is not a good Republican idea, it's not a good Democrat idea, it's simply an American idea, and they need to get their work done."

— ARGONNE NATIONAL LABORATORY, ILLINOIS, JULY 22, 2002

"And I must say, relations with Congress are a heck of a lot better than they have been in the past, because congressmen and senators of both parties are interested [in] doing right for the American people."

— AT A TOWN HALL MEETING IN ORLANDO, FLORIDA,
DECEMBER 4, 2001

"And when they end up helping somebody who's been on welfare, they realize they're more help than the person they're trying to help."

—IN A RUSH TO WRAP UP A SPEECH ON WELFARE REFORM
AT THE WHITE HOUSE ON APRIL 18, 2002

"You know what's interesting about Washington? It's the kind of place where second-guessing has become second nature."

—MAY 17, 2002

"[Like] your question implies, it would be nice to have had the bill done yesterday. But sometimes democracy doesn't work quite that fast."

—IN RESPONSE TO A QUESTION ABOUT DELAYS ON
THE PASSAGE OF THE AVIATION BILL,
WASHINGTON, D.C., NOVEMBER 9, 2001

"As we say down home, there's no bull about [the Alaskan senator Ted Stevens]. That's good for the Senate, that's good for the people of Alaska, and, more importantly, it's good for the United States of America."

—WASHINGTON, D.C., MAY 9, 2002

His Address to the Nation

SEPTEMBER 11, 2001

Good evening. Today, our fellow citizens, our way of life, our very freedom came under attack in a series of deliberate and deadly terrorist acts. The victims were in airplanes, or in their offices; secretaries, businessmen and -women, military and federal workers; moms and dads, friends and neighbors. Thousands of lives were suddenly ended by evil, despicable acts of terror.

The pictures of airplanes flying into buildings, fires burning, huge structures collapsing, have filled us with disbelief, terrible sadness, and a quiet, unyielding anger. These acts of mass murder were intended to frighten our nation into chaos and retreat. But they have failed; our country is strong.

A great people has been moved to defend a great nation. Terrorist attacks can shake the foundations of our biggest buildings, but they cannot touch the foundation of America. These acts shattered steel, but they cannot dent the steel of American resolve.

America was targeted for attack because we're the brightest beacon for freedom and opportunity in the world. And no one will keep that light from shining.

Today, our nation saw evil, the very worst of human nature. And we responded with the best of America—with the daring of our rescue workers, with the caring for strangers and neighbors who came to give blood and help in any way they could.

Immediately following the first attack, I implemented our government's emergency response plans. Our military is powerful, and it's prepared. Our emergency teams are working in New York City and Washington, D.C., to help with local rescue efforts.

Our first priority is to get help to those who have been injured, and to take every precaution to protect our citizens at home and around the world from further attacks.

The functions of our government continue without interruption. Federal agencies in Washington, which had to be evacuated today, are reopening for essential personnel tonight, and will be open for business tomorrow. Our financial institutions remain strong, and the American economy will be open for business, as well.

The search is under way for those who are behind these evil acts. I've directed the full resources of our intelligence and law enforcement communities to find those responsible and to bring them to justice. We will make no distinction between the terrorists who committed these acts and those who harbor them.

I appreciate so very much the members of Congress who have joined me in strongly condemning these attacks. And on behalf of the American people, I thank the many world leaders who have called to offer their condolences and assistance.

America and our friends and allies join with all those who want peace and security in the world, and we stand together to win the war against terrorism. Tonight, I ask for your prayers for all those who grieve, for the children whose worlds have been shattered, for all whose sense of safety and security has been threatened. And I pray they will be comforted by a power greater than any of us, spoken through the ages in Psalm 23: "Even though I walk through the valley of the shadow of death, I fear no evil, for You are with me."

This is a day when all Americans from every walk of life unite in our resolve for justice and peace. America has stood down enemies before, and we will do so this time. None of us will ever forget this day. Yet, we go forward to defend freedom and all that is good and just in our world.

Thank you. Good night, and God bless America.

On Terrorists

"[For] a generation leading up to September the 11th, 2001, terrorists and their radical allies attacked innocent people in the Middle East and beyond, without facing a sustained and serious response. The terrorists became convinced that free nations were decadent and weak. And they grew bolder, believing that history was on their side. Since America put out the fires of September the 11th, and mourned our dead, and went to war, history has taken a different turn. We have carried the fight to the enemy. We are rolling back the terrorist threat to civilization, not on the fringes of its influence, but at the heart of its power."

—Address to the nation, September 7, 2003

"People say, 'How can I help on this war against terror? How can I fight evil?' You can do so by mentoring a child; by going into a shut-in's house and say I love you."

—Washington, D.C., September 19, 2002

"For America, there will be no going back to the era before September the 11th, 2001—to false comfort in a dangerous world. We have learned that terrorist attacks are not caused by the use of strength; they are invited by the perception of weakness."
—Washington, D.C., September 7, 2003

"Listen, we're a great nation. We welcome people in. We just want to know why you're here. And if you're not supposed to be here more than a period of time, then maybe you ought to just go on home."
—New York City, New York, February 6, 2002

"Two years ago, I told the Congress and the country that the war on terror would be a lengthy war, a different kind of war, fought on many fronts in many places. Iraq is now the central front. Enemies of freedom are making a desperate stand there—and there they must be defeated. This will take time and require sacrifice. Yet we will do what is necessary, we will spend what is necessary, to achieve this essential victory in the war on terror, to promote freedom, and to make our own nation more secure."
—Address to the nation, September 7, 2003

"If America goes to sleep, the rest of the world is in trouble. If we blink, the rest of the world will close their eyes. So we're not blinking, and we're not going to sleep."
—Los Angeles, California, April 29, 2002

"Shadowy terrorists could hook up with a nation that has got weapons of mass destruction, the nations that I labeled axis of evil, people who in one case have gassed their own people with weapons of mass destruction."

—KANSAS CITY, MISSOURI, JUNE 11, 2002

"President Musharraf, he's still tight with us on the war against terror, and that's what I appreciate. . . . He understands that we've got to keep al Qaeda on the run, and that by keeping him on the run, it's more likely we will bring him to justice."

—RUCH, OREGON, AUGUST 22, 2002

"When I take action, I'm not going to fire a two-million-dollar missile at a ten-dollar empty tent and hit a camel in the butt. It's going to be decisive."

—*NEWSWEEK*, SEPTEMBER 24, 2001

"I urge the leaders in Europe and around the world to take swift, decisive action against terror groups such as Hamas, to cut off their funding and support, as the United States has done."

—WASHINGTON, D.C., JUNE 25, 2003

His Address to a Joint Session of Congress

SEPTEMBER 21, 2001

Mr. Speaker, Mr. President Pro Tempore, members of Congress, and fellow Americans: In the normal course of events, presidents come to this chamber to report on the state of the union. Tonight, no such report is needed. It has already been delivered by the American people.

We have seen it in the courage of passengers, who rushed terrorists to save others on the ground—passengers like an exceptional man named Todd Beamer. And would you please help me to welcome his wife, Lisa Beamer, here tonight?

We have seen the state of our union in the endurance of rescuers, working past exhaustion. We have seen the unfurling of flags, the lighting of candles, the giving of blood, the saying of prayers—in English, Hebrew, and Arabic. We have seen the decency of a loving and giving people who have made the grief of strangers their own.

My fellow citizens, for the last nine days, the entire world has seen for itself the state of our union—and it is strong.

Tonight we are a country awakened to danger and called to defend freedom. Our grief has turned to anger, and anger to resolution. Whether we bring our enemies to justice, or bring justice to our enemies, justice will be done.

I thank the Congress for its leadership at such an important time. All of America was touched on the evening of the tragedy to see Republicans and Democrats joined together on the steps of this Capitol, singing "God Bless America." And you did more than sing; you acted, by delivering $40 billion to rebuild our communities and meet the needs of our military.

Speaker Hastert, Minority Leader Gephardt, Majority Leader Daschle, and Senator Lott, I thank you for your friendship, for your leadership, and for your service to our country.

And on behalf of the American people, I thank the world for its outpouring of support. America will never forget the sounds of our national anthem playing at Buckingham Palace, on the streets of Paris, and at Berlin's Brandenburg Gate.

We will not forget South Korean children gathering to pray outside our embassy in Seoul, or the prayers of sympathy offered at a mosque in Cairo. We will not forget moments of silence and days of mourning in Australia and Africa and Latin America.

Nor will we forget the citizens of eighty other nations who died with our own: dozens of Pakistanis; more than 130 Israelis; more than 250 citizens of India; men and women from El Salvador, Iran, Mexico, and Japan; and hundreds of British citizens. America has no truer friend than Great Britain. Once again, we are joined together in a great cause—so honored the British prime minister has crossed an ocean to show his unity of purpose with America. Thank you for coming, friend.

On September the 11th, enemies of freedom committed an act of war against our country. Americans have known wars—but for the past 136 years, they have been wars on foreign soil, except for one Sunday in 1941. Americans have known the casualties of war—but not at the center of a great city on a peaceful morning. Americans have known surprise attacks—but never before on thousands of civilians. All of this was brought upon us in a single day—and night fell on a different world, a world where freedom itself is under attack.

Americans have many questions tonight. Americans are asking: Who attacked our country? The evidence we have gathered all points to a collection of loosely affiliated terrorist organizations known as al Qaeda. They are the same murderers indicted for bombing American embassies in Tanzania and Kenya, and responsible for bombing the USS *Cole*.

Al Qaeda is to terror what the Mafia is to crime. But its goal is not making money; its goal is remaking the world—and imposing its radical beliefs on people everywhere.

The terrorists practice a fringe form of Islamic extremism that has been rejected by Muslim scholars and the vast majority of Muslim clerics—a fringe movement that perverts the peaceful teachings of Islam. The terrorists' directive commands them to kill Christians and Jews, to kill all Americans, and make no distinction among military and civilians, including women and children.

This group and its leader—a person named Osama bin Laden—are linked to many other organizations in different countries, including the Egyptian Islamic Jihad and the Islamic

Movement of Uzbekistan. There are thousands of these terrorists in more than sixty countries. They are recruited from their own nations and neighborhoods and brought to camps in places like Afghanistan, where they are trained in the tactics of terror. They are sent back to their homes or sent to hide in countries around the world to plot evil and destruction.

The leadership of al Qaeda has great influence in Afghanistan and supports the Taliban regime in controlling most of that country. In Afghanistan, we see al Qaeda's vision for the world.

Afghanistan's people have been brutalized—many are starving and many have fled. Women are not allowed to attend school. You can be jailed for owning a television. Religion can be practiced only as their leaders dictate. A man can be jailed in Afghanistan if his beard is not long enough.

The United States respects the people of Afghanistan—after all, we are currently its largest source of humanitarian aid—but we condemn the Taliban regime. It is not only repressing its own people, it is threatening people everywhere by sponsoring and sheltering and supplying terrorists. By aiding and abetting murder, the Taliban regime is committing murder.

And tonight, the United States of America makes the following demands on the Taliban: Deliver to United States authorities all the leaders of al Qaeda who hide in your land. Release all foreign nationals, including American citizens, you have unjustly imprisoned. Protect foreign journalists, diplomats, and aid workers in your country. Close immediately and permanently every terrorist training camp in Afghanistan, and hand over every terrorist, and every person in their support structure, to appropriate authorities. Give the United States full access to terrorist training camps, so we can make sure they are no longer operating.

These demands are not open to negotiation or discussion. The Taliban must act, and act immediately. They will hand over the terrorists, or they will share in their fate.

I also want to speak tonight directly to Muslims throughout the world. We respect your faith. It's practiced freely by many millions of Americans, and by millions more in countries that America counts as friends. Its teachings are good and peaceful, and those who commit evil in the name of Allah blaspheme the name of Allah. The terrorists are traitors to their own faith, trying, in effect, to hijack Islam itself. The enemy of America is not our many Muslim friends; it is not our many Arab friends. Our enemy is a radical network of terrorists, and every government that supports them.

Our war on terror begins with al Qaeda, but it does not end there. It will not end until every terrorist group of global reach has been found, stopped, and defeated.

Americans are asking, why do they hate us? They hate what we see right here in this chamber—a democratically elected government. Their leaders are self-appointed. They hate our freedoms—our freedom of religion, our freedom of speech, our freedom to vote and assemble and disagree with each other.

They want to overthrow existing governments in many Muslim countries, such as Egypt, Saudi Arabia, and Jordan. They want to drive Israel out of the Middle East. They want to drive Christians and Jews out of vast regions of Asia and Africa.

These terrorists kill not merely to end lives, but to disrupt and end a way of life. With every atrocity, they hope that America grows fearful, retreating from the world and forsaking our friends. They stand against us, because we stand in their way.

We are not deceived by their pretenses to piety. We have seen their kind before. They are the heirs of all the murderous ideologies of the twentieth century. By sacrificing human life to serve their radical visions—by abandoning every value except the will to power—they follow in the path of fascism, and Nazism, and totalitarianism. And they will follow that path all the way, to where it ends: in history's unmarked grave of discarded lies.

Americans are asking: How will we fight and win this war? We will direct every resource at our command—every means of diplomacy, every tool of intelligence, every instrument of law enforcement, every financial influence, and every necessary weapon of war—to the disruption and to the defeat of the global terror network.

This war will not be like the war against Iraq a decade ago, with a decisive liberation of territory and a swift conclusion. It will not look like the air war above Kosovo two years ago, where no ground troops were used and not a single American was lost in combat.

Our response involves far more than instant retaliation and isolated strikes. Americans should not expect one battle, but a lengthy campaign, unlike any other we have ever seen. It may include dramatic strikes, visible on TV, and covert operations, secret even in success. We will starve terrorists of funding, turn them one against another, drive them from place to place, until there is no refuge or no rest. And we will pursue nations that provide aid or safe haven to terrorism. Every nation, in every region, now has a decision to make. Either you are with us, or you are with the terrorists. From this day forward, any nation that continues to harbor or support terrorism will be regarded by the United States as a hostile regime.

Our nation has been put on notice: We are not immune from attack. We will take defensive measures against terrorism to protect Americans. Today, dozens of federal departments and agencies, as well as state and local governments, have responsibilities affecting homeland security. These efforts must be coordinated at the highest level. So tonight I announce the creation of a Cabinet-level position reporting directly to me— the Office of Homeland Security.

And tonight I also announce a distinguished American to lead this effort, to strengthen American security: a military veteran, an effective governor, a true patriot, a trusted friend— Pennsylvania's Tom Ridge. He will lead, oversee, and coordinate a comprehensive national strategy to safeguard our country against terrorism and respond to any attacks that may come.

These measures are essential. But the only way to defeat terrorism as a threat to our way of life is to stop it, eliminate it, and destroy it where it grows.

Many will be involved in this effort, from FBI agents to intelligence operatives to the reservists we have called to active duty. All deserve our thanks, and all have our prayers. And tonight, a few miles from the damaged Pentagon, I have a message for our military: Be ready. I've called the armed forces to alert, and there is a reason. The hour is coming when America will act, and you will make us proud.

This is not, however, just America's fight. And what is at stake is not just America's freedom. This is the world's fight. This is civilization's fight. This is the fight of all who believe in progress and pluralism, tolerance and freedom.

We ask every nation to join us. We will ask, and we will need, the help of police forces, intelligence services, and banking systems around the world. The United States is grateful that many nations and many international organizations have already responded—with sympathy and with support. Nations from Latin America, to Asia, to Africa, to Europe, to the Islamic world. Perhaps the NATO Charter reflects best the attitude of the world: An attack on one is an attack on all.

The civilized world is rallying to America's side. They understand that if this terror goes unpunished, their own cities, their own citizens may be next. Terror, unanswered, cannot only bring down buildings, it can threaten the stability of legitimate governments. And you know what—we're not going to allow it.

Americans are asking: What is expected of us? I ask you to live your lives, and hug your children. I know many citizens have fears tonight, and I ask you to be calm and resolute, even in the face of a continuing threat.

I ask you to uphold the values of America, and remember why so many have come here. We are in a fight for our principles, and our first responsibility is to live by them. No one should be singled out for unfair treatment or unkind words because of their ethnic background or religious faith.

I ask you to continue to support the victims of this tragedy with your contributions. Those who want to give can go to a central source of information, libertyunites.org, to find the names of groups providing direct help in New York, Pennsylvania, and Virginia.

The thousands of FBI agents who are now at work in this investigation may need your cooperation, and I ask you to give it.

I ask for your patience with the delays and inconveniences that may accompany tighter security, and for your patience in what will be a long struggle.

I ask your continued participation and confidence in the American economy. Terrorists attacked a symbol of American prosperity. They did not touch its source. America is successful because of the hard work and creativity and enterprise of our people. These were the true strengths of our economy before September 11th, and they are our strengths today.

And, finally, please continue praying for the victims of terror and their families, for those in uniform, and for our great country. Prayer has comforted us in sorrow and will help strengthen us for the journey ahead.

Tonight I thank my fellow Americans for what you have already done and for what you will do. And, ladies and gentlemen of the Congress, I thank you, their representatives, for what you have already done and for what we will do together.

Tonight, we face new and sudden national challenges. We will come together to improve air safety, to dramatically expand the number of air marshals on domestic flights, and take new measures to prevent hijacking. We will come together to promote stability and keep our airlines flying, with direct assistance during this emergency.

We will come together to give law enforcement the additional tools it needs to track down terror here at home. We will come together to strengthen our intelligence capabilities to know the plans of terrorists before they act and find them before they strike.

We will come together to take active steps that strengthen America's economy and put our people back to work.

Tonight we welcome two leaders who embody the extraordinary spirit of all New Yorkers: Governor George Pataki and Mayor Rudolph Giuliani. As a symbol of America's resolve, my administration will work with Congress, and these two leaders, to show the world that we will rebuild New York City.

After all that has just passed—all the lives taken and all the possibilities and hopes that died with them—it is natural to wonder if America's future is one of fear. Some speak of an age of terror. I know there are struggles ahead, and dangers to face. But this country will define our times, not be defined by them. As long as the United States of America is determined and strong, this will not be an age of terror; this will be an age of liberty, here and across the world.

Great harm has been done to us. We have suffered great loss. And in our grief and anger we have found our mission and our moment. Freedom and fear are at war. The advance of human freedom—the great achievement of our time, and the great hope of every time—now depends on us. Our nation—this generation—will lift a dark threat of violence from our people and our future. We will rally the world to this cause by our efforts, by our courage. We will not tire, we will not falter, and we will not fail.

It is my hope that in the months and years ahead, life will return almost to normal. We'll go back to our lives and routines, and that is good. Even grief recedes with time and grace. But our resolve must not pass. Each of us will remember what happened that day, and to whom it happened. We'll remember the moment the news came—where we were and what we were doing. Some will remember an image of a fire or a story of rescue. Some will carry memories of a face and a voice gone forever.

And I will carry this: It is the police shield of a man named George Howard, who died at the World Trade Center trying to save others. It was given to me by his mom, Arlene, as a proud memorial to her son. This is my reminder of lives that ended, and a task that does not end.

I will not forget this wound to our country or those who inflicted it. I will not yield; I will not rest; I will not relent in waging this struggle for freedom and security for the American people.

The course of this conflict is not known, yet its outcome is certain. Freedom and fear, justice and cruelty, have always been at war, and we know that God is not neutral between them.

Fellow citizens, we'll meet violence with patient justice— assured of the rightness of our cause and confident of the victories to come. In all that lies before us, may God grant us wisdom, and may He watch over the United States of America.

Thank you.

On Family

"I'm sorry the first lady is not here with me—she's hiking. But I can't tell you how proud I am of her. She's doing a fabulous job as the first lady of the United States."

— CHARLESTON, SOUTH CAROLINA, JULY 29, 2002

"As president, I will work to build a culture that respects life."

— ON ABORTION, SEPTEMBER 29, 2000

"A strong America is America based upon strong families."

— GREEN TREE, PENNSYLVANIA, AUGUST 5, 2002

"It solved my biggest political problem in Texas. There's no question about it, and I knew it all along. My problem was 'What's the boy ever done?' I have to make a fairly large splash in the pool in order for people to recognize me. My pool has been expanded so much because of who my dad is. The advantage is that everybody knows who I am. The disadvantage is that no matter how great my accomplishments may be, no one is going to give me credit for them."

— ON OWNING THE TEXAS RANGERS,
AS REPORTED IN *FIRST SON* BY BILL MINUTAGLIO

"I'm really proud of Laura. . . . She didn't care for politics and didn't particularly like politicians. Now she's stuck with one. And she's doing a fabulous job as first lady."

— LITTLE ROCK, ARKANSAS, AUGUST 29, 2002

"If we are going to save a generation of young people, our children must know they will face bad consequences for criminal behavior. Sadly, too many youths are not getting that message. Our juvenile justice system must say to our children: We love you, but we are going to hold you accountable for your actions."

— FROM THE BUSH CAMPAIGN LITERATURE

"He went to Greenwich Country Day School, and I went to San Jacinto Junior High."

— WHEN ASKED WHAT MADE HIM DIFFERENT FROM
HIS FAMOUS FATHER, AS REPORTED IN
FIRST SON BY BILL MINUTAGLIO

"Today, through sonograms and other technology, we can . . . see clearly that unborn children are members of the human family, as well. They reflect our image, and they are created in God's own image."

— PITTSBURGH, PENNSYLVANIA, AUGUST 5, 2002

"It's hard to believe, but—I don't have time to worry about being George Bush's son. Maybe it's a result of being confident. I'm not sure how the psychoanalysts will analyze it, but I'm not worried about it. I'm really not. I'm a free guy."

— *FIRST SON* BY BILL MINUTAGLIO

"Skeptics say, 'Governor, if you take away our licenses, we won't be able to earn a living to pay child support.' To those parents, I have a simple response: 'Pay up.'"

— FROM HIS STATE OF THE STATE ADDRESS,
AUSTIN, TEXAS, FEBRUARY 7, 1995

"If you are a mom and dad, you are responsible for loving your child with all your heart and all your soul."

— FROM REMARKS AT THE REPUBLICAN RETREAT LUNCHEON,
WHITE SULPHUR SPRINGS, WEST VIRGINIA,
FEBRUARY 1, 2002

"And above all, we welcome the Eisenhower family, and send our good wishes to John Eisenhower, who could not be with us today. As the son of a president myself, I know how proud John must feel, knowing that our country's respect for his father has only increased with the years."

— WASHINGTON, D.C., MAY 7, 2002

His Address to the Nation on the Use of Force in Afghanistan

OCTOBER 7, 2001

Good afternoon. On my orders, the United States military has begun strikes against al Qaeda terrorist training camps and military installations of the Taliban regime in Afghanistan. These carefully targeted actions are designed to disrupt the use of Afghanistan as a terrorist base of operations and to attack the military capability of the Taliban regime.

We are joined in this operation by our staunch friend, Great Britain. Other close friends, including Canada, Australia, Germany, and France, have pledged forces as the operation unfolds. More than forty countries in the Middle East, Africa,

Europe, and across Asia have granted air transit or landing rights. Many more have shared intelligence. We are supported by the collective will of the world.

More than two weeks ago, I gave Taliban leaders a series of clear and specific demands: Close terrorist training camps; hand over leaders of the al Qaeda network; and return all foreign nationals, including American citizens, unjustly detained in your country. None of these demands were met. And now the Taliban will pay a price. By destroying camps and disrupting communications, we will make it more difficult for the terror network to train new recruits and coordinate their evil plans.

Initially, the terrorists may burrow deeper into caves and other entrenched hiding places. Our military action is also designed to clear the way for sustained, comprehensive, and relentless operations to drive them out and bring them to justice.

At the same time, the oppressed people of Afghanistan will know the generosity of America and our allies. As we strike military targets, we'll also drop food, medicine, and supplies to the starving and suffering men and women and children of Afghanistan.

The United States of America is a friend to the Afghan people, and we are the friends of almost a billion worldwide who practice the Islamic faith. The United States of America is an enemy of those who aid terrorists and of the barbaric criminals who profane a great religion by committing murder in its name.

This military action is a part of our campaign against terrorism, another front in a war that has already been joined through diplomacy, intelligence, the freezing of financial assets, and the arrests of known terrorists by law enforcement agents in thirty-eight countries. Given the nature and reach of our enemies, we will win this conflict by the patient accumulation of successes, by meeting a series of challenges with determination and will and purpose.

Today we focus on Afghanistan, but the battle is broader. Every nation has a choice to make. In this conflict, there is no neutral ground. If any government sponsors the outlaws and killers of innocents, they have become outlaws and murderers themselves. And they will take that lonely path at their own peril.

I'm speaking to you today from the Treaty Room of the White House, a place where American presidents have worked for peace. We're a peaceful nation. Yet, as we have learned, so suddenly and so tragically, there can be no peace in a world of sudden terror. In the face of today's new threat, the only way to pursue peace is to pursue those who threaten it.

We did not ask for this mission, but we will fulfill it. The name of today's military operation is Enduring Freedom. We defend not only our precious freedoms, but also the freedom of people everywhere to live and raise their children free from fear.

I know many Americans feel fear today. And our government is taking strong precautions. All law enforcement and intelligence agencies are working aggressively around America, around the world, and around the clock. At my request, many governors have activated the National Guard to strengthen airport security. We have called up reserves to reinforce our military capability and strengthen the protection of our homeland.

In the months ahead, our patience will be one of our strengths—patience with the long waits that will result from tighter security; patience and understanding that it will take time to achieve our goals; patience in all the sacrifices that may come.

Today, those sacrifices are being made by members of our Armed Forces who now defend us so far from home, and by their proud and worried families. A commander-in-chief sends America's sons and daughters into a battle in a foreign land only after the greatest care and a lot of prayer. We ask a lot of those who wear our uniform. We ask them to leave their loved ones, to travel great distances, to risk injury, even to be prepared to make the ultimate sacrifice of their lives. They are dedicated, they are honorable; they represent the best of our country. And we are grateful.

To all the men and women in our military—every sailor, every soldier, every airman, every coastguardsman, every Marine—I say this: Your mission is defined; your objectives are clear; your goal is just. You have my full confidence, and you will have every tool you need to carry out your duty.

I recently received a touching letter that says a lot about the state of America in these difficult times—a letter from a fourth-grade girl, with a father in the military: "As much as I don't want my dad to fight," she wrote, "I'm willing to give him to you."

This is a precious gift, the greatest she could give. This young girl knows what America is all about. Since September 11, an entire generation of young Americans has gained new understanding of the value of freedom, and its cost in duty and in sacrifice.

The battle is now joined on many fronts. We will not waver; we will not tire; we will not falter; and we will not fail. Peace and freedom will prevail.

Thank you. May God continue to bless America.

On War

"The heaviest burdens in our war on terror fall, as always, on the men and women of our armed forces and our intelligence services. They have removed gathering threats to America and our friends, and this nation takes great pride in their incredible achievements. We are grateful for their skill and courage, and for their acts of decency, which have shown America's character to the world. We honor the sacrifice of their families. And we mourn every American who has died so bravely, so far from home."

— WASHINGTON, D.C., SEPTEMBER 7, 2003

"The deliberate and deadly attacks which were carried out yesterday against our country were more than acts of terror. They were acts of war."

— ADDRESS FROM CABINET ROOM
FOLLOWING CABINET MEETING, SEPTEMBER 12, 2001

"Since the end of major combat operations [in Iraq], we have conducted raids seizing many caches of enemy weapons and massive amounts of ammunition, and we have captured or killed hundreds of Saddam loyalists and terrorists. So far, of the 55 most wanted former Iraqi leaders, 42 are dead or in custody. We are sending a clear message: Anyone who seeks to harm our soldiers can know that our soldiers are hunting for them."

—WASHINGTON, D.C., SEPTEMBER 7, 2003

"There is a certain sense of fascination with previous wars in Kosovo and Desert Storm, where people could turn on their TV screens and see high-tech weaponry burrowing into bunkers and massive explosions."

—WASHINGTON, D.C., OCTOBER 9, 2001

"The culture in our agencies have changed. We are now interested in preventing attack."

—FROM REMARKS MADE TO BUSINESS, TRADE, AND AGRICULTURE LEADERS IN THE EAST ROOM, WASHINGTON, D.C., OCTOBER 26, 2001

On Foreign Relations

"One year ago, the people of Afghanistan lived under oppression. Their country was a haven for terror. Today, they're an . . . emerging democracy, and building a better future."

— The White House, September 10, 2002

"This foreign policy stuff is a little frustrating."

— New York Daily News, April 23, 2002

"The American people appreciate Ireland's work . . . to help secure passage of Resolution 1441. . . . We appreciate [their] own support for ensuring that the just demands of the world are enforced."

— The White House, March 13, 2003

"The Middle East will either become a place of progress and peace, or it will be an exporter of violence and terror that takes more lives in America and in other free nations."

— Address to the nation, September 7, 2003

"And so one of the areas where I think the average Russian will realize that the stereotypes of America have changed is that it's a spirit of cooperation, not one-upmanship."

—CRAWFORD HIGH SCHOOL, CRAWFORD, TEXAS,
NOVEMBER 15, 2001

"I want the United Nations to be effective. It's important for it to be a robust, capable body. It's important for its words to mean what they say, and as we head into the twenty-first century, Mark, when it comes to our security, we really don't need anybody's permission."

—RESPONDING TO A REPORTER AT A PRIME-TIME
PRESS CONFERENCE, THE WHITE HOUSE, MARCH 6, 2003

"Show the world you respect Cuban citizens enough to listen to your citizens and count their votes."

—CHALLENGING CUBA'S GOVERNMENT ON FREE ELECTIONS,
WASHINGTON, D.C., MAY 20, 2002

"I talked about the visit to Poland and to Russia, where we've got good friends in both those countries."

—WASHINGTON, D.C., JUNE 9, 2003

"Iran would be dangerous if they have a nuclear weapon."

—WASHINGTON, D.C., JUNE 18, 2003

"The fundamental question is, 'Will I be a successful president when it comes to foreign policy?' I will be."

—WAYNE, MICHIGAN, JUNE 28, 2000,
AS QUOTED BY KATHARINE Q. SEELYE IN THE *NEW YORK TIMES*

"You're the kind of guy I like to have in a foxhole with me."
— A COMMENT MADE TO THE RUSSIAN PRESIDENT
VLADIMIR PUTIN, THE WHITE HOUSE, NOVEMBER 13, 2001

"I understand that the unrest in the Middle East creates unrest throughout the region."
— WASHINGTON, D.C., MARCH 13, 2002

"Part of the problem in dealing with North Korea [is that] we're not certain as to whether or not they're keeping all terms of all agreements."
— WASHINGTON, D.C., MARCH 15, 2001

"We're looking at border policies, both with Canada and with Mexico. And we'll continue doing what we're doing now."
— CRAWFORD, TEXAS, DECEMBER 31, 2001

"Syria just needs to know we expect full cooperation. And that we strongly urge them not to allow for Baath Party members or Saddam's families or generals on the run to seek safe haven and find safe haven there. We expect them to do everything they can to prevent people who should be held to account from escaping in their country. And if they are in their country, we expect the Syrian authorities to turn them over to the proper folks."
— BETHESDA, MARYLAND, APRIL 11, 2003

"I look forward to seeing [Tony Blair] at Checquers. And we sat next to each other at my first EU luncheon—NATO luncheon—anyway, at the first luncheon with leaders I sat next to

Tony. It was very comforting to sit next to a friend, kind of the new boy in class, you know—sat next to a friend. And he's easy to talk to, which is a high compliment when it comes from a Texan."

— FROM A BBC INTERVIEW, JULY 20, 2001

"I also challenge Cuba's government to ease its stranglehold . . . on private economic activity."

— THE WHITE HOUSE, MAY 20, 2002

"There's nothing more deep than recognizing Israel's right to exist. . . . I can't think of anything more deep than that right."

— WASHINGTON, D.C., MARCH 13, 2002

"Border relations between Canada and Mexico have never been better."

— FROM A PRESS CONFERENCE WITH
THE CANADIAN PRIME MINISTER, SEPTEMBER 24, 2001

"We must understand that the . . . decisions to make the area more secure must be made in the context of peace for the long run."

— FROM A PRESS CONFERENCE WITH
KING ABDULLAH OF JORDAN, AUGUST 1, 2002

"Hello, Landslide!"

— GREETING BRITISH PRIME MINISTER TONY BLAIR
AFTER BLAIR WON REELECTION BY A LANDSLIDE,
WASHINGTON, D.C., JUNE 20, 2001

"Every life matters, whether it be an American life or the life of an Afghan girl."

— LITTLE ROCK, ARKANSAS, AUGUST 29, 2002

"We share a vision of two states, Israel and Palestine, living side by side in peace."

— *NEW YORK TIMES*, APRIL 6, 2002

"[The North Korean leader Kim Jong Il is] starving his own people . . . [and imprisoning intellectuals in] a gulag the size of Houston."

— FROM A PRIVATE MEETING WITH REPUBLICAN SENATORS,
WASHINGTON, D.C., MAY 16, 2002,
AS REPORTED IN *NEWSWEEK*, MAY 27, 2002

"I confirmed to the prime minister that we appreciate our friendship."

— SAID AFTER MEETING WITH CANADIAN PRIME MINISTER
JEAN CHRÉTIEN, FEBRUARY 5, 2001

"I'm a patient man. But I haven't changed my opinion since the last time [King Abdullah of Jordan] was in the Oval Office. And one of the things we will do is consult with our friends."

— THE WHITE HOUSE, JULY 31, 2002

"The other day—somebody asked me one time, a while ago, they said, 'Has he [Chairman Arafat] disappointed you, has he lost your respect?' I said, 'Well, he hasn't earned my respect yet.'"

— CRAWFORD, TEXAS, APRIL 28, 2002

"Mexico is an incredibly important part of the *futuro de los Estados Unidos*."

—EL PASO, TEXAS, MARCH 21, 2002

"Secondly, I had a chance to speak to the United Nations to talk about another threat . . . that we face—all of us face—in the civilized world, and that is a threat of weapons of mass destruction in the hands of leaders who disregard human liberty, [who] do not believe in freedom."

—WHILE TALKING ABOUT SADDAM HUSSEIN WITH REPORTERS AND ITALIAN PRIME MINISTER BERLUSCONI, CAMP DAVID, MARYLAND, SEPTEMBER 14, 2002

"There are . . . a lot of Palestinians who wonder whether or not life is worth living. And we've got, as a world, have got to help them understand there is a positive life ahead for them and their children."

—CRAWFORD, TEXAS, APRIL 28, 2002

"Russia is no longer our enemy and therefore we shouldn't be locked into a Cold War mentality that says we keep the peace by blowing each other up. In my attitude, that's old, that's tired, that's stale."

—DES MOINES, IOWA, JUNE 8, 2001

"I think the operative question is, how soon will you start working on reforms? . . . The answer is, as soon as possible. That's what we discussed about—how quickly can we begin the reform process."

—FROM A MEETING WITH ISRAELI PRIME MINISTER ARIEL SHARON, WASHINGTON, D.C., MAY 7, 2002

"And today, I'm informing the prime minister that we're lifting the travel ban on Turkey."

—WHILE IN A PRESS CONFERENCE WITH
TURKISH PRIME MINISTER BULENT ECEVIT,
JANUARY 16, 2002

"I assured the prime minister of Canada that my vision of the hemisphere goes both north and south."

—WHILE TALKING TO REPORTERS ABOARD
AIR FORCE ONE, FEBRUARY 13, 2001

"So there's a lot we can find with these world leaders that you've got in common with them, if you just spend some time listening."

—TEXAS STATE TECHNICAL COLLEGE AIRPORT,
WACO, TEXAS, NOVEMBER 14, 2001

"If Russia thought that the neighborhood was unsettled, it might create some issues. But Poland has provided a great source of stability in the neighborhood and, therefore, Russia feels less threatened. And I think that's an important nuance, as we say, in foreign policy."

—FROM A PRESS CONFERENCE WITH THE PRESIDENT OF POLAND,
THE WHITE HOUSE, JULY 17, 2002

"But the true threats to stability and peace are these nations that [have . . .] authoritarian regimes."

—FROM A MEDIA ROUNDTABLE,
WASHINGTON, D.C., MARCH 13, 2001

"After all, a week ago, there were—Yasser Arafat was boarded up in his building in Ramallah, a building full of, evidently,

German peace protestors and all kinds of people. They're now out. He's now free to show leadership."

—THE WHITE HOUSE, WASHINGTON, D.C., MAY 2, 2002

"And as to how to achieve that vision [of peace] is something we must consult with our friends."

—DURING A MEETING WITH
CROWN PRINCE ABDALLAH OF SAUDI ARABIA,
CRAWFORD, TEXAS, APRIL 25, 2002

His Second State of
the Union Address

JANUARY 29, 2002

Mr. Speaker, Vice President Cheney, members of Congress, distinguished guests, fellow citizens: As we gather tonight, our nation is at war, our economy is in recession, and the civilized world faces unprecedented dangers. Yet the state of our union has never been stronger.

We last met in an hour of shock and suffering. In four short months, our nation has comforted the victims; begun to rebuild New York and the Pentagon; rallied a great coalition; captured, arrested, and rid the world of thousands of terrorists; destroyed Afghanistan's terrorist training camps; saved a people from starvation; and freed a country from brutal oppression.

The American flag flies again over our embassy in Kabul. Terrorists who once occupied Afghanistan now occupy cells at

Guantánamo Bay. And terrorist leaders who urged followers to sacrifice their lives are running for their own.

America and Afghanistan are now allies against terror. We'll be partners in rebuilding that country. And this evening we welcome the distinguished interim leader of a liberated Afghanistan: Chairman Hamid Karzai.

The last time we met in this chamber, the mothers and daughters of Afghanistan were captives in their own homes, forbidden from working or going to school. Today women are free and are part of Afghanistan's new government. And we welcome the new minister of women's affairs, Dr. Sima Samar.

Our progress is a tribute to the spirit of the Afghan people, to the resolve of our coalition, and to the might of the United States military. When I called our troops into action, I did so with complete confidence in their courage and skill. And tonight, thanks to them, we are winning the war on terror. The men and women of our armed forces have delivered a message now clear to every enemy of the United States: Even seven thousand miles away, across oceans and continents, on mountaintops and in caves—you will not escape the justice of this nation.

For many Americans, these four months have brought sorrow and pain that will never completely go away. Every day a retired firefighter returns to Ground Zero, to feel closer to his two sons who died there. At a memorial in New York, a little boy left his football with a note for his lost father: "Dear Daddy, please take this to heaven. I don't want to play football until I can play with you again some day."

Last month, at the grave of her husband, Michael, a CIA officer and Marine who died in Mazur-e-Sharif, Shannon Spann said these words of farewell: "Semper Fi, my love." Shannon is with us tonight.

Shannon, I assure you and all who have lost a loved one that our cause is just, and our country will never forget the debt we owe Michael and all who gave their lives for freedom.

Our cause is just, and it continues. Our discoveries in Afghanistan confirmed our worst fears and showed us the true scope of the task ahead. We have seen the depth of our enemies' hatred in videos, where they laugh about the loss of innocent life. And the depth of their hatred is equaled by the madness of the destruction they design. We have found diagrams of American nuclear power plants and public water facilities, detailed instructions for making chemical weapons, surveillance maps of American cities, and thorough descriptions of landmarks in America and throughout the world.

What we have found in Afghanistan confirms that, far from ending there, our war against terror is only beginning. Most of the nineteen men who hijacked planes on September the 11th were trained in Afghanistan's camps, and so were tens of thousands of others. Thousands of dangerous killers, schooled in the methods of murder, often supported by outlaw regimes, are now spread throughout the world like ticking time bombs, set to go off without warning.

Thanks to the work of our law enforcement officials and coalition partners, hundreds of terrorists have been arrested. Yet, tens of thousands of trained terrorists are still at large. These enemies view the entire world as a battlefield, and we must pursue them wherever they are. So long as training camps operate, so long as nations harbor terrorists, freedom is at risk. And America and our allies must not, and will not, allow it.

Our nation will continue to be steadfast and patient and persistent in the pursuit of two great objectives. First, we will shut down terrorist camps, disrupt terrorist plans, and bring terrorists to justice. And, second, we must prevent the terrorists and regimes who seek chemical, biological, or nuclear weapons from threatening the United States and the world.

Our military has put the terror training camps of Afghanistan out of business, yet camps still exist in at least a dozen countries. A terrorist underworld—including groups like Hamas, Hezbollah, Islamic Jihad, Jaish-i-Mohammed—operates in remote jungles and deserts, and hides in the centers of large cities.

While the most visible military action is in Afghanistan, America is acting elsewhere. We now have troops in the Philippines, helping to train that country's armed forces to go after terrorist cells that have executed an American and still hold hostages. Our soldiers, working with the Bosnian government, seized terrorists who were plotting to bomb our embassy. Our navy is patrolling the coast of Africa to block the shipment of weapons and the establishment of terrorist camps in Somalia.

My hope is that all nations will heed our call and eliminate the terrorist parasites who threaten their countries and our own. Many nations are acting forcefully. Pakistan is now cracking down on terror, and I admire the strong leadership of President Musharraf.

But some governments will be timid in the face of terror. And make no mistake about it: If they do not act, America will.

Our second goal is to prevent regimes that sponsor terror from threatening America or our friends and allies with weapons of mass destruction. Some of these regimes have been pretty quiet since September the 11th. But we know their true nature. North Korea is a regime arming with missiles and weapons of mass destruction, while starving its citizens.

Iran aggressively pursues these weapons and exports terror, while an unelected few repress the Iranian people's hope for freedom.

Iraq continues to flaunt its hostility toward America and to support terror. The Iraqi regime has plotted to develop anthrax and nerve gas and nuclear weapons for over a decade. This is a regime that has already used poison gas to murder thousands of its own citizens—leaving the bodies of mothers huddled over their dead children. This is a regime that agreed to international inspections—then kicked out the inspectors. This is a regime that has something to hide from the civilized world.

States like these, and their terrorist allies, constitute an axis of evil, arming to threaten the peace of the world. By seeking weapons of mass destruction, these regimes pose a grave and growing danger. They could provide these arms to terrorists, giving them the means to match their hatred. They could attack our allies or attempt to blackmail the United States. In any of these cases, the price of indifference would be catastrophic.

We will work closely with our coalition to deny terrorists and their state sponsors the materials, technology, and expertise to make and deliver weapons of mass destruction. We will develop and deploy effective missile defenses to protect America and our allies from sudden attack. And all nations should know: America will do what is necessary to ensure our nation's security.

We'll be deliberate, yet time is not on our side. I will not wait on events, while dangers gather. I will not stand by, as peril draws closer and closer. The United States of America will not permit the world's most dangerous regimes to threaten us with the world's most destructive weapons.

Our war on terror is well begun, but it is only begun. This campaign may not be finished on our watch—yet it must be and it will be waged on our watch.

We can't stop short. If we stop now—leaving terror camps intact and terror states unchecked—our sense of security would be false and temporary. History has called America and our allies to action, and it is both our responsibility and our privilege to fight freedom's fight.

Our first priority must always be the security of our nation, and that will be reflected in the budget I send to Congress. My budget supports three great goals for America: We will win this war; we'll protect our homeland; and we will revive our economy.

September the 11th brought out the best in America, and the best in this Congress. And I join the American people in applauding your unity and resolve. Now Americans deserve to have this same spirit directed toward addressing problems here at home. I'm a proud member of my party—yet as we act to win the war, protect our people, and create jobs in America, we must act, first and foremost, not as Republicans, not as Democrats, but as Americans.

It costs a lot to fight this war. We have spent more than a billion dollars a month—over $30 million a day—and we must be prepared for future operations. Afghanistan proved that expensive precision weapons defeat the enemy and spare innocent lives, and we need more of them. We need to replace aging aircraft and make our military more agile, to put our troops anywhere in the world quickly and safely. Our men and women in uniform deserve the best weapons, the best equipment, the best training—and they also deserve another pay raise.

My budget includes the largest increase in defense spending in two decades—because while the price of freedom and security is high, it is never too high. Whatever it costs to defend our country, we will pay.

The next priority of my budget is to do everything possible to protect our citizens and strengthen our nation against the ongoing threat of another attack. Time and distance from the events of September the 11th will not make us safer unless we act on its lessons. America is no longer protected by vast oceans. We are protected from attack only by vigorous action abroad and increased vigilance at home.

My budget nearly doubles funding for a sustained strategy of homeland security, focused on four key areas: bioterrorism, emergency response, airport and border security, and improved intelligence. We will develop vaccines to fight anthrax and other deadly diseases. We'll increase funding to help states and communities train and equip our heroic police and firefighters. We will improve intelligence collection and sharing, expand patrols at our borders, strengthen the security of air travel, and use technology to track the arrivals and departures of visitors to the United States.

Homeland security will make America not only stronger but, in many ways, better. Knowledge gained from bioterrorism research will improve public health. Stronger police and fire departments will mean safer neighborhoods. Stricter border enforcement will help combat illegal drugs. And as government works to better secure our homeland, America will continue to depend on the eyes and ears of alert citizens.

A few days before Christmas, an airline flight attendant spotted a passenger lighting a match. The crew and passengers quickly subdued the man, who had been trained by al Qaeda and was armed with explosives. The people on that plane were alert and, as a result, likely saved nearly two hundred lives. And tonight we welcome and thank flight attendants Hermis Moutardier and Christina Jones.

Once we have funded our national security and our homeland security, the final great priority of my budget is economic security for the American people. To achieve these great national objectives—to win the war, protect the homeland, and revitalize our economy—our budget will run a deficit that will be small and short-term, so long as Congress restrains spending and acts in a fiscally responsible manner. We have clear priorities and we must act at home with the same purpose and resolve we have shown overseas: We'll prevail in the war, and we will defeat this recession.

Americans who have lost their jobs need our help, and I support extending unemployment benefits and direct assistance for health care coverage. Yet, American workers want more than unemployment checks—they want a steady paycheck. When America works, America prospers, so my economic security plan can be summed up in one word: jobs.

Good jobs begin with good schools, and here we've made a fine start. Republicans and Democrats worked together to achieve historic education reform so that no child is left behind. I was proud to work with members of both parties: Chairman John Boehner and Congressman George Miller. Senator Judd Gregg. And I was so proud of our work, I even had nice things to say about my friend, Ted Kennedy. I know the folks at the Crawford coffee shop couldn't believe I'd say such a thing—but our work on this bill shows what is possible if we set aside posturing and focus on results.

There is more to do. We need to prepare our children to read and succeed in school with improved Head Start and early childhood development programs. We must upgrade our teacher colleges and teacher training and launch a major recruiting drive with a great goal for America: a quality teacher in every classroom.

Good jobs also depend on reliable and affordable energy. This Congress must act to encourage conservation, promote technology, build infrastructure, and it must act to increase energy production at home so America is less dependent on foreign oil.

Good jobs depend on expanded trade. Selling into new markets creates new jobs, so I ask Congress to finally approve trade promotion authority. On these two key issues, trade and energy, the House of Representatives has acted to create jobs, and I urge the Senate to pass this legislation.

Good jobs depend on sound tax policy. Last year, some in this hall thought my tax relief plan was too small; some thought it was too big. But when the checks arrived in the mail, most Americans thought tax relief was just about right. Congress listened to the people and responded by reducing tax rates, doubling the child credit, and ending the death tax. For the sake of long-term growth and to help Americans plan for the future, let's make these tax cuts permanent.

The way out of this recession, the way to create jobs, is to grow the economy by encouraging investment in factories and equipment, and by speeding up tax relief so people have more money to spend. For the sake of American workers, let's pass a stimulus package.

Good jobs must be the aim of welfare reform. As we reauthorize these important reforms, we must always remember the goal is to reduce dependency on government and offer every American the dignity of a job.

Americans know economic security can vanish in an instant without health security. I ask Congress to join me this year to enact a patients' bill of rights to give uninsured workers credits to help buy health coverage, to approve an historic increase in the spending for veterans' health, and to give seniors a sound and modern Medicare system that includes coverage for prescription drugs.

A good job should lead to security in retirement. I ask Congress to enact new safeguards for 401(k) and pension plans. Employees who have worked hard and saved all their lives should not have to risk losing everything if their company fails. Through stricter accounting standards and tougher disclosure requirements, corporate America must be made more accountable to employees and shareholders and held to the highest standards of conduct.

Retirement security also depends upon keeping the commitments of Social Security, and we will. We must make Social Security financially stable and allow personal retirement accounts for younger workers who choose them.

Members, you and I will work together in the months ahead on other issues: productive farm policy, a cleaner environment, broader home ownership, especially among minorities, and ways to encourage the good work of charities and faith-based groups. I ask you to join me on these important domestic issues in the same spirit of cooperation we've applied to our war against terrorism.

During these last few months, I've been humbled and privileged to see the true character of this country in a time of testing. Our enemies believed America was weak and materialistic, that we would splinter in fear and selfishness. They were as wrong as they are evil.

The American people have responded magnificently, with courage and compassion, strength and resolve. As I have met the heroes, hugged the families, and looked into the tired faces of rescuers, I have stood in awe of the American people.

And I hope you will join me—I hope you will join me in expressing thanks to one American for the strength and calm and comfort she brings to our nation in crisis, our first lady, Laura Bush.

None of us would ever wish the evil that was done on September the 11th. Yet, after America was attacked, it was as if our entire country looked into a mirror and saw our better selves. We were reminded that we are citizens, with obligations to each other, to our country, and to history. We began to think less of the goods we can accumulate and more about the good we can do.

For too long our culture has said, "If it feels good, do it." Now America is embracing a new ethic and a new creed: "Let's roll." In the sacrifice of soldiers, the fierce brotherhood of firefighters, and the bravery and generosity of ordinary citizens, we have glimpsed what a new culture of responsibility could look like. We want to be a nation that serves goals larger than self. We've been offered a unique opportunity, and we must not let this moment pass.

My call tonight is for every American to commit at least two years—four thousand hours over the rest of your lifetime—to the service of your neighbors and your nation. Many are already serving, and I thank you. If you aren't sure how to help, I've got a good place to start. To sustain and extend the best that has emerged in America, I invite you to join the new USA Freedom Corps. The Freedom Corps will focus on three areas of need: responding in case of crisis at home; rebuilding our communities; and extending American compassion throughout the world.

One purpose of the USA Freedom Corps will be homeland security. America needs retired doctors and nurses who can be mobilized in major emergencies; volunteers to help police and fire departments; transportation and utility workers well-trained in spotting danger.

Our country also needs citizens working to rebuild our communities. We need mentors to love children, especially children whose parents are in prison. And we need more talented teachers in troubled schools. USA Freedom Corps will expand and improve the good efforts of AmeriCorps and Senior Corps to recruit more than 200,000 new volunteers.

And America needs citizens to extend the compassion of our country to every part of the world. So we will renew the promise of the Peace Corps, double its volunteers over the next five years, and ask it to join a new effort to encourage development and education and opportunity in the Islamic world.

This time of adversity offers a unique moment of opportunity—a moment we must seize to change our culture. Through the gathering momentum of millions of acts of service and decency and kindness, I know we can overcome evil with greater good. And we have a great opportunity during this time of war to lead the world toward the values that will bring lasting peace.

All fathers and mothers, in all societies, want their children to be educated, and live free from poverty and violence. No people on earth yearn to be oppressed or aspire to servitude or eagerly await the midnight knock of the secret police.

If anyone doubts this, let them look to Afghanistan, where the Islamic "street" greeted the fall of tyranny with song and celebration. Let the skeptics look to Islam's own rich history, with its centuries of learning and tolerance and progress. America will lead by defending liberty and justice because they are right and true and unchanging for all people everywhere.

No nation owns these aspirations, and no nation is exempt from them. We have no intention of imposing our culture. But America will always stand firm for the nonnegotiable demands of human dignity: the rule of law; limits on the power of the state; respect for women; private property; free speech; equal justice; and religious tolerance.

America will take the side of brave men and women who advocate these values around the world, including the Islamic world, because we have a greater objective than eliminating threats and containing resentment. We seek a just and peaceful world beyond the war on terror.

In this moment of opportunity, a common danger is erasing old rivalries. America is working with Russia and China and India, in ways we have never before, to achieve peace and prosperity. In every region, free markets and free trade and free societies are proving their power to lift lives. Together with friends and allies from Europe to Asia, and Africa to Latin America, we will demonstrate that the forces of terror cannot stop the momentum of freedom.

The last time I spoke here, I expressed the hope that life would return to normal. In some ways, it has. In others, it never will. Those of us who have lived through these challenging times have been changed by them. We've come to know truths that we will never question: Evil is real, and it must be opposed. Beyond all differences of race or creed, we are one country, mourning together and facing danger together. Deep in the American character, there is honor, and it is stronger than cynicism. And many have discovered again that even in tragedy— especially in tragedy—God is near.

In a single instant, we realized that this will be a decisive decade in the history of liberty, that we've been called to a unique role in human events. Rarely has the world faced a choice more clear or consequential.

Our enemies send other people's children on missions of suicide and murder. They embrace tyranny and death as a cause and a creed. We stand for a different choice, made long ago, on the day of our founding. We affirm it again today. We choose freedom and the dignity of every life.

Steadfast in our purpose, we now press on. We have known freedom's price. We have shown freedom's power. And in this great conflict, my fellow Americans, we will see freedom's victory.

Thank you all. May God bless.

On History

"I loved history and pursued a diversified course of study. I like to think of it as the academic road less traveled. For example, I took a class that studied Japanese haiku. Haiku, for the uninitiated, is a fifteenth-century form of poetry, each poem having seventeen syllables. Haiku is fully understood only by the Zen masters. As I recall, one of my academic advisers was worried about my selection of such a specialized course. He said I should focus on English. I still hear that quite often. But my critics don't realize I don't make verbal gaffes. I'm speaking in the perfect forms and rhythms of ancient haiku."

—Yale University, New Haven, Connecticut, May 21, 2001

"Listen, history has called us to action. I don't want to be in a position where we look back and say, 'Why didn't they lead, where were they when it came to our basic freedoms?' And we are going to lead."

—From a press conference with German Chancellor Gerhardt Schroeder, Berlin, Germany, May 23, 2002

"There is such hope here in Northern Ireland that the past can be broken."

— BELFAST, NORTHERN IRELAND, APRIL 8, 2003

"After all, we're at war, and for the first time in our nation's history, part of the battlefront is here at home. . . . This is a very unusual period in American history, obviously. We've never been attacked like this before. We're still being attacked. Our heart goes out to anybody who suffers in America. And so, we're bolstering our homeland defense. We're disrupting and denying anybody who wants to harm the American people."

— FROM REMARKS TO THE NATIONAL ASSOCIATION OF MANUFACTURERS, OCTOBER 31, 2002

"It seems odd that with all the history it contains, this great building went more than a century without a name befitting its dignity. We've solved that problem today, and we've solved it once and for all. This building now bears the name of Dwight D. Eisenhower."

— WASHINGTON, D.C., MAY 7, 2002

"History has called us into action. History has laid the mantle of responsibility for peace squarely on our shoulders. I accept that responsibility, and so does the American people."

— SANTA CLARA, CALIFORNIA, MAY 1, 2002

"When we grew up, the baby boomers and everybody else, we never really thought we'd be attacked. I mean, the last thing that I entered my mind when I was getting out of high school in 1964 is that an enemy would attack America."

— EDEN PRAIRIE, MINNESOTA, MARCH 4, 2002

"I want the youngsters here to remember the story of Flight 93, one of the most profound parts of . . . the recent history we've been through."

— St. Louis, Missouri, November 4, 2002

"We do believe this is the first time a president has been out of the country for Memorial Day."

— Paris, France, May 26, 2002

"Twenty-eight percent of eighth-graders do not know the reason why the Civil War was fought."

— The White House, September 17, 2002

"Like the Nazis and the communists before them, the terrorists seek to end lives and control all life. And like the Nazis and the communists before them, they will be opposed by free nations and the terrorists will be defeated."

— Vilnius, Lithuania, November 23, 2002

"And all our history says we believe in liberty and justice for all . . . that when we see oppression, we cry."

— East Literature Magnet School,
Nashville, Tennessee, September 17, 2002

"I had the privilege of voting in the Republican primary in 1974. As you know, you've got a one-month residency requirement [in Alaska]—and I met it. So I voted . . . I was a proud participant."

— Anchorage, Alaska, February 16, 2002

"I think that one of the greatest contributions of Poland to our country is Polish Americans—people who are enterprising, hardworking, God-fearing, family-loving people. One of the great strengths of our country is our diversity."

— The White House, January 14, 2003

"There wasn't a lot of protest at Yale in '68. I don't remember that. And I think most people—I don't know if you found anything differently—I just don't remember any great days of rage. I think those were mainly in the '70s."

— New York Times, June 19, 2000

"There's no doubt in my mind that when it's all said and done the facts will show the world the truth. There's going to be, you know, a lot of attempts to try to rewrite history, and I can understand that. But I'm absolutely confident in the decision I made [to go to war in Iraq]."

— Pretoria, South Africa, July 9, 2003

"There was war on other continents, but we were safe."

— On America before the September 11 attacks, Washington, D.C., February 10, 2003

On the Media

"If I answer questions every time you ask one, expectations would be high. And as you know, I like to keep expectations low."
— Washington, D.C., December 10, 2002

"It's important for those of us who value democracy to promote an independent media."
— Moscow, Russia, May 24, 2002

"I know how to handle the press."
— *First Son* by Bill Minutaglio

"We live in a culture of moral indifference, where movies and videos glamorize violence and tolerance is touted as a great virtue."
— Texas A&M University, College Station, Texas, April 6, 1998

"I'm very gracious and humbled."
— To Cokie Roberts, *This Week*, February 20, 2000

"I'm not going to talk about what I did as a child. . . . What's relevant is that I have learned from any mistakes I made."
— FROM AN INTERVIEW WITH WMUR-TV IN NEW HAMPSHIRE,
WHEN ASKED IF HE HAD USED "DRUGS, MARIJUANA, COCAINE"

"Well, it got my attention this morning when I read about [the Immigration and Naturalization Services' inadvertently approving visas for two terrorists]. I was stunned, and not happy. Let me put it another way—I was plenty hot."
— WHITE HOUSE PRESS CONFERENCE, MARCH 13, 2002

"I don't want to hold two press conferences in one week."
— MARCH 20, 2002

"People make suggestions on what to say all the time. I'll give you an example: I don't read what's handed to me. People say, 'Here, here's your speech, or here's an idea for a speech.' They're changed. Trust me."
— FROM AN INTERVIEW WITH THE *NEW YORK TIMES*,
MARCH 15, 2000

"Listen, it's a healthy debate for people to express their opinion. People should be allowed to express their opinion. But America needs to know, I'll be making up my mind based upon the latest intelligence and how best to protect our own country plus our friends and allies."
— CRAWFORD, TEXAS, AUGUST 16, 2002

"Put the 'off' button on."
— SUGGESTING A SOLUTION FOR PARENTS
WANTING TO CURB FOUL LANGUAGE AND VIOLENCE
ON TV, SOUTH CAROLINA, FEBRUARY 14, 2000

"I read the newspaper."

—Response to a question about his reading habits
during the New Hampshire Republican debate
on December 2, 1999

"I've seen this before. I'm a guy whose father was called a 'wimp' on the cover of *Newsweek* the day he declared his race for the presidency. If it gets too bad, I'll let you know. I damn sure will let *Newsweek* know."

—*First Son* by Bill Minutaglio

On the TV program *Meet the Press* on November 21, 1999, reporter Tim Russert had the following exchange with then-governor Bush.

RUSSERT: If someone came to you and said, "Governor, I'm sorry, I'm going to go public with some information." What do you do?

GOVERNOR BUSH: If someone was willing to go public with information that was damaging, you'd have heard about it by now. You'd had heard about it now. My background has been scrutinized by all kinds of reporters. Tim, we can talk about this all morning.

"John, we're going to get a good bill. I mean, one of the things I've learned is not to try to negotiate . . . on national TV."

—To reporter John King
in a CNN interview, April 25, 2001

"I thought how proud I am to be standing up beside my dad. Never did it occur to me that he would become the gist for cartoonists."

—*Newsweek*, February 28, 2000

His Third State of the Union Address

JANUARY 28, 2003

M r. Speaker, Vice President Cheney, members of Congress, distinguished guests, fellow citizens: Every year, by law and by custom, we meet here to consider the state of the union. This year, we gather in this chamber deeply aware of decisive days that lie ahead.

You and I serve our country in a time of great consequence. During this session of Congress, we have the duty to reform domestic programs vital to our country, and we have the opportunity to save millions of lives abroad from a terrible disease. We will work for a prosperity that is broadly shared, and we will answer every danger and every enemy that threatens the American people.

In all these days of promise and days of reckoning, we can be confident. In a whirlwind of change and hope and peril, our faith is sure, our resolve is firm, and our union is strong.

This country has many challenges. We will not deny, we will not ignore, we will not pass along our problems to other Congresses, other presidents, and other generations. We will confront them with focus and clarity and courage.

During the last two years, we have seen what can be accomplished when we work together. To lift the standards of our public schools, we achieved historic education reform—which must now be carried out in every school, and every classroom, so that every child in America can read and learn and succeed in life. To protect our country, we reorganized our government and created the Department of Homeland Security—which is mobilizing against the threats of a new era. To bring our economy out of recession, we delivered the largest tax relief in a generation. To insist on integrity in American business, we passed tough reforms, and we are holding corporate criminals to account.

Some might call this a good record. I call it a good start. Tonight I ask the House and Senate to join me in the next bold steps to serve our fellow citizens.

Our first goal is clear: We must have an economy that grows fast enough to employ every man and woman who seeks a job.

After recession, terrorist attacks, corporate scandals, and stock market declines, our economy is recovering—yet it is not growing fast enough, or strongly enough. With unemployment rising, our nation needs more small businesses to open, more companies to invest and expand, more employers to put up the sign that says, "Help Wanted."

Jobs are created when the economy grows; the economy grows when Americans have more money to spend and invest; and the best, fairest way to make sure Americans have that money is not to tax it away in the first place.

I am proposing that all the income tax reductions set for 2004 and 2006 be made permanent and effective this year. And under my plan, as soon as I have signed the bill, this extra money will start showing up in workers' paychecks. Instead of gradually reducing the marriage penalty, we should do it now. Instead of slowly raising the child credit to $1,000, we should send the checks to American families now.

This tax relief is for everyone who pays income taxes—and it will help our economy immediately. Ninety-two million Americans will keep—this year—an average of almost $1,100 more of their own money. A family of four with an income of $40,000 would see their federal income taxes fall from $1,178 to $45 per year. And our plan will improve the bottom line for more than 23 million small businesses.

You, the Congress, have already passed all these reductions and promised them for future years. If this tax relief is good for Americans three, or five, or seven years from now, it is even better for Americans today.

We also strengthen the economy by treating investors equally in our tax laws. It is fair to tax a company's profits. It is not fair to again tax the shareholder on the same profits. To boost investor confidence, and to help the nearly 10 million seniors who receive dividend income, I ask you to end the unfair double taxation of dividends.

Lower taxes and greater investment will help this economy expand. More jobs mean more taxpayers—and higher revenues to our government. The best way to address the deficit and move toward a balanced budget is to encourage economic growth—and to show some spending discipline in Washington, D.C. We must work together to fund only our most important priorities. I will send you a budget that increases discretionary spending by four percent next year—about as much as the average family's income is expected to grow. And that is a good benchmark for us: Federal spending should not rise any faster than the paychecks of American families.

A growing economy and a focus on essential priorities will also be crucial to the future of Social Security. As we continue to work together to keep Social Security sound and reliable, we must offer younger workers a chance to invest in retirement accounts that they will control and they will own.

Our second goal is high-quality, affordable health care for all Americans. The American system of medicine is a model of skill and innovation—with a pace of discovery that is adding good years to our lives. Yet for many people, medical care costs too much—and many have no coverage at all. These problems will not be solved with a nationalized health care system that dictates coverage and rations care.

Instead, we must work toward a system in which all Americans have a good insurance policy, choose their own doctors, and seniors and low-income Americans receive the help they need. Instead of bureaucrats and trial lawyers and HMOs, we must put doctors and nurses and patients back in charge of American medicine.

Health care reform must begin with Medicare, because Medicare is the binding commitment of a caring society. We must renew that commitment by giving seniors access to the preventive medicine and new drugs that are transforming health care in America.

Seniors happy with the current Medicare system should be able to keep their coverage just the way it is. And just like you, the members of Congress, members of your staffs, and other federal employees, all seniors should have the choice of a health care plan that provides prescription drugs. My budget will commit an additional $400 billion over the next decade to reform and strengthen Medicare. Leaders of both political parties have talked for years about strengthening Medicare— I urge the members of this new Congress to act this year.

To improve our health care system, we must address one of the prime causes of higher costs—the constant threat that physicians and hospitals will be unfairly sued. Because of excessive litigation, everybody pays more for health care—and many parts of America are losing fine doctors. No one has ever been healed by a frivolous lawsuit—and I urge the Congress to pass medical liability reform.

Our third goal is to promote energy independence for our country, while dramatically improving the environment. I have sent you a comprehensive energy plan to promote energy efficiency and conservation, to develop cleaner technology, and to produce more energy at home. I have sent you Clear Skies legislation that mandates a 70 percent cut in air pollution from power plants over the next fifteen years. I have sent you a Healthy Forests Initiative, to help prevent the catastrophic fires that devastate communities, kill wildlife, and burn away millions of acres of treasured forest.

I urge you to pass these measures, for the good of both our environment and our economy. Even more, I ask you to take a crucial step and protect our environment in ways that generations before us could not have imagined.

In this century, the greatest environmental progress will

come about not through endless lawsuits or command-and-control regulations, but through technology and innovation. Tonight I am proposing $1.2 billion in research funding so that America can lead the world in developing clean, hydrogen-powered automobiles.

A simple chemical reaction between hydrogen and oxygen generates energy, which can be used to power a car—producing only water, not exhaust fumes. With a new national commitment, our scientists and engineers will overcome obstacles to taking these cars from laboratory to showroom—so that the first car driven by a child born today could be powered by hydrogen, and pollution-free. Join me in this important innovation—to make our air significantly cleaner, and our country much less dependent on foreign sources of energy.

Our fourth goal is to apply the compassion of America to the deepest problems of America. For so many in our country—the homeless, the fatherless, the addicted—the need is great. Yet there is power—wonder-working power—in the goodness, and idealism, and faith of the American people.

Americans are doing the work of compassion every day—visiting prisoners, providing shelter to battered women, bringing companionship to lonely seniors. These good works deserve our praise; they deserve our personal support; and, when appropriate, they deserve the assistance of our government. I urge you to pass both my faith-based initiative and the Citizen Service Act—to encourage acts of compassion that can transform America, one heart and one soul at a time.

Last year, I called on my fellow citizens to participate in USA Freedom Corps, which is enlisting tens of thousands of new volunteers across America. Tonight I ask Congress and the American people to focus the spirit of service and the resources of government on the needs of some of our most vulnerable citizens—boys and girls trying to grow up without guidance and attention, and children who have to go through a prison gate to be hugged by their mom or dad.

I propose a $450 million initiative to bring mentors to more than a million disadvantaged junior high students and children of prisoners. Government will support the training and recruiting of mentors, yet it is the men and women of America who will fill the need. One mentor, one person, can change a life forever—and I urge you to be that one person.

Another cause of hopelessness is addiction to drugs. Addiction crowds out friendship, ambition, moral conviction, and reduces all the richness of life to a single destructive desire. As a government, we are fighting illegal drugs by cutting off supplies, and reducing demand through antidrug education programs. Yet for those already addicted, the fight against drugs is a fight for their own lives. Too many Americans in search of treatment cannot get it. So tonight I propose a new $600 million program to help an additional 300,000 Americans receive treatment over the next three years.

Our nation is blessed with recovery programs that do amazing work. One of them is found at the Healing Place Church in Baton Rouge, Louisiana. A man in the program said, "God does miracles in people's lives, and you never think it could be you." Tonight, let us bring to all Americans who struggle with drug addiction this message of hope: The miracle of recovery is possible, and it could be you.

By caring for children who need mentors, and for addicted men and women who need treatment, we are building a more welcoming society—a culture that values every life. And in this work we must not overlook the weakest among us. I ask you to protect infants at the very hour of birth, and end the practice of partial-birth abortion. And because no human life should be started or ended as the object of an experiment, I ask you to set a high standard for humanity and pass a law against all human cloning.

The qualities of courage and compassion that we strive for in America also determine our conduct abroad. The American flag stands for more than our power and our interests. Our founders dedicated this country to the cause of human dignity— the rights of every person and the possibilities of every life. This conviction leads us into the world to help the afflicted, and defend the peace, and confound the designs of evil men. In Afghanistan, we helped to liberate an oppressed people, and we will continue helping them secure their country, rebuild their society, and educate all their children—boys and girls. In the Middle East, we will continue to seek peace between a secure Israel and a democratic Palestine. Across the earth, America is feeding the hungry; more than 60 percent of international food aid comes as a gift from the people of the United States.

As our nation moves troops and builds alliances to make our world safer, we must also remember our calling, as a blessed country, to make this world better. Today, on the continent of Africa, nearly thirty million people have the AIDS virus— including three million children under the age of fifteen. There are whole countries in Africa where more than one-third of the adult population carries the infection. More than four million require immediate drug treatment. Yet across that continent, only fifty thousand AIDS victims—only fifty thousand—are receiving the medicine they need.

Because the AIDS diagnosis is considered a death sentence, many do not seek treatment. Almost all who do are turned away. A doctor in rural South Africa describes his frustration. He says, "We have no medicines . . . many hospitals tell [people], 'You've got AIDS. We can't help you. Go home and die.'"

In an age of miraculous medicines, no person should have to hear those words. AIDS can be prevented. Anti-retroviral drugs can extend life for many years. And the cost of those drugs has dropped from $12,000 a year to under $300 a year—which places a tremendous possibility within our grasp.

Ladies and gentlemen, seldom has history offered a greater opportunity to do so much for so many. We have confronted, and will continue to confront, HIV/AIDS in our own country. And to meet a severe and urgent crisis abroad, tonight I propose the Emergency Plan for AIDS Relief—a work of mercy beyond all current international efforts to help the people of Africa. This comprehensive plan will prevent 7 million new AIDS infections, treat at least 2 million people with life-extending drugs, and provide humane care for millions of people suffering from AIDS, and for children orphaned by AIDS. I ask the Congress to commit $15 billion over the next five years, including nearly $10 billion in new money, to turn the tide against AIDS in the most afflicted nations of Africa and the Caribbean.

This nation can lead the world in sparing innocent people from a plague of nature. And this nation is leading the world in confronting and defeating the man-made evil of international terrorism.

There are days when the American people do not hear news about the war on terror. There is never a day when I do not learn of another threat, or receive reports of operations in progress, or give an order in this global war against a scattered network of killers. The war goes on, and we are winning.

To date we have arrested, or otherwise dealt with, many key commanders of al Qaeda. They include a man who directed logistics and funding for the September 11th attacks, the chief of al Qaeda operations in the Persian Gulf who planned the bombings of our embassies in East Africa and the USS *Cole*, an al Qaeda operations chief from Southeast Asia, a former director of al Qaeda's training camps in Afghanistan, a key al Qaeda operative in Europe, and a major al Qaeda leader in Yemen. All told, more than three thousand suspected terrorists have been arrested in many countries. And many others have met a different fate. They are no longer a problem for the United States and our friends and allies.

We are working closely with other nations to prevent further attacks. America and coalition countries have uncovered and stopped terrorist conspiracies targeting the American embassy in Yemen, the American embassy in Singapore, a Saudi military base, and ships in the Straits of Hormuz and the Straits of Gibraltar. We have broken al Qaeda cells in Hamburg and Milan and Madrid and London and Paris—as well as Buffalo, New York.

We have the terrorists on the run, and we are keeping them on the run. One by one, the terrorists are learning the meaning of American justice.

As we fight this war, we will remember where it began—here, in our own country. This government is taking unprecedented measures to protect our people and defend our homeland. We have intensified security at the borders and ports of entry, posted more than fifty thousand newly trained federal screeners in airports, begun inoculating troops and first responders against smallpox, and are deploying the nation's first early warning network of sensors to detect biological attack. And this year, for the first time, we are beginning to field a defense to protect this nation against ballistic missiles.

I thank the Congress for supporting these measures. I ask you tonight to add to our future security with a major research and production effort to guard our people against bioterrorism, called Project Bioshield. The budget I send you will propose almost $6 billion to quickly make available effective vaccines and treatments against agents like anthrax, botulinum toxin, Ebola, and plague. We must assume that our enemies would use these diseases as weapons, and we must act before the dangers are upon us.

Since September 11th, our intelligence and law enforcement agencies have worked more closely than ever to track and disrupt the terrorists. The FBI is improving its ability to analyze intelligence, and transforming itself to meet new threats. And tonight, I am instructing the leaders of the FBI, the CIA, the Homeland Security, and the Department of Defense to develop a Terrorist Threat Integration Center to merge and analyze all threat information in a single location. Our government must have the very best information possible, and we will use it to make sure the right people are in the right places to protect our citizens.

Our war against terror is a contest of will in which perseverance is power. In the ruins of two towers, at the western wall of the Pentagon, on a field in Pennsylvania, this nation made a pledge, and we renew that pledge tonight: Whatever the duration of this struggle, and whatever the difficulties, we will not permit the triumph of violence in the affairs of men—free people will set the course of history.

Today, the gravest danger in the war on terror—the gravest danger facing America and the world—is outlaw regimes that seek and possess nuclear, chemical, and biological weapons. These regimes could use such weapons for blackmail, terror, and mass murder. They could also give or sell those weapons to their terrorist allies, who would use them without the least hesitation.

This threat is new; America's duty is familiar. Throughout the twentieth century, small groups of men seized control of great nations, built armies and arsenals, and set out to dominate the weak and intimidate the world. In each case, their ambitions of cruelty and murder had no limit. In each case, the ambitions of Hitlerism, militarism, and communism were defeated by the will of free peoples, by the strength of great alliances, and by the might of the United States of America. Now, in this century, the ideology of power and domination has appeared again and seeks to gain the ultimate weapons of terror. Once again, this nation and our friends are all that stand between a world at peace, and a world of chaos and constant alarm. Once again, we are called to defend the safety of our people, and the hopes of all mankind. And we accept this responsibility.

America is making a broad and determined effort to confront these dangers. We have called on the United Nations to fulfill its charter and stand by its demand that Iraq disarm. We are strongly supporting the International Atomic Energy Agency in its mission to track and control nuclear materials around the world. We are working with other governments to secure nuclear materials in the former Soviet Union and to strengthen global treaties banning the production and shipment of missile technologies and weapons of mass destruction.

In all of these efforts, however, America's purpose is more than to follow a process—it is to achieve a result: the end of terrible threats to the civilized world. All free nations have a stake in preventing sudden and catastrophic attack. We are asking them to join us, and many are doing so. Yet the course of this nation does not depend on the decisions of others. Whatever action is required, whenever action is necessary, I will defend the freedom and security of the American people.

Different threats require different strategies. In Iran, we continue to see a government that represses its people, pursues weapons of mass destruction, and supports terror. We also see Iranian citizens risking intimidation and death as they speak out for liberty, human rights, and democracy. Iranians, like all people, have a right to choose their own government and determine their own destiny—and the United States supports their aspirations to live in freedom.

On the Korean peninsula, an oppressive regime rules a people living in fear and starvation. Throughout the 1990s, the United States relied on a negotiated framework to keep North Korea from gaining nuclear weapons. We now know that the regime was deceiving the world and developing those weapons all along. And today the North Korean regime is using its nuclear program to incite fear and seek concessions. America and the world will not be blackmailed. America is working with the countries of the region—South Korea, Japan, China, and Russia—to find a peaceful solution and to show the North Korean government that nuclear weapons will bring only isolation, economic stagnation, and continued hardship. The North Korean regime will find respect in the world, and revival for its people, only when it turns away from its nuclear ambitions.

Our nation and the world must learn the lessons of the Korean peninsula and not allow an even greater threat to rise up in Iraq. A brutal dictator, with a history of reckless aggression, with ties to terrorism, with great potential wealth, will not be permitted to dominate a vital region and threaten the United States.

Twelve years ago, Saddam Hussein faced the prospect of being the last casualty in a war he had started and lost. To spare himself, he agreed to disarm of all weapons of mass destruction. For the next twelve years, he systematically violated that agreement. He pursued chemical, biological, and nuclear weapons even while inspectors were in his country. Nothing to date has restrained him from his pursuit of these weapons—not economic sanctions, not isolation from the civilized world, not even cruise missile strikes on his military facilities.

Almost three months ago, the United Nations Security Council gave Saddam Hussein his final chance to disarm. He has shown instead his utter contempt for the United Nations, and for the opinion of the world.

The 108 U.N. weapons inspectors were not sent to conduct a scavenger hunt for hidden materials across a country the size of California. The job of the inspectors is to verify that Iraq's regime is disarming. It is up to Iraq to show exactly where it is hiding its banned weapons, lay those weapons out for the world to see, and destroy them as directed. Nothing like this has happened.

The United Nations concluded in 1999 that Saddam Hussein had biological weapons materials sufficient to produce over twenty-five thousand liters of anthrax—enough doses to kill several million people. He has not accounted for that material. He has given no evidence that he has destroyed it.

The United Nations concluded that Saddam Hussein had materials sufficient to produce more than thirty-eight thousand liters of botulinum toxin—enough to subject millions of people to death by respiratory failure. He has not accounted for that material. He has given no evidence that he has destroyed it.

Our intelligence officials estimate that Saddam Hussein had the materials to produce as much as five hundred tons of sarin, mustard, and VX nerve agent. In such quantities, these chemical agents also could kill untold thousands. He has not accounted for these materials. He has given no evidence that he has destroyed them.

U.S. intelligence indicates that Saddam Hussein had upwards of thirty thousand munitions capable of delivering chemical agents. Inspectors recently turned up sixteen of them, despite Iraq's recent declaration denying their existence. Saddam Hussein has not accounted for the remaining 29,984 of these prohibited munitions. He has given no evidence that he has destroyed them.

From three Iraqi defectors we know that Iraq, in the late 1990s, had several mobile biological weapons labs. These are designed to produce germ warfare agents and can be moved from place to place to evade inspectors. Saddam Hussein has not disclosed these facilities. He has given no evidence that he has destroyed them.

The International Atomic Energy Agency confirmed in the 1990s that Saddam Hussein had an advanced nuclear weapons development program, had a design for a nuclear weapon, and was working on five different methods of enriching uranium for a bomb. The British government has learned that Saddam Hussein recently sought significant quantities of uranium from Africa. Our intelligence sources tell us that he has attempted to purchase high-strength aluminum tubes suitable for nuclear weapons production. Saddam Hussein has not credibly explained these activities. He clearly has much to hide.

The dictator of Iraq is not disarming. To the contrary, he is deceiving. From intelligence sources, we know, for instance, that thousands of Iraqi security personnel are at work hiding documents and materials from the U.N. inspectors—sanitizing inspection sites and monitoring the inspectors themselves. Iraqi officials accompany the inspectors in order to intimidate witnesses. Iraq is blocking U-2 surveillance flights requested by the United Nations. Iraqi intelligence officers are posing as the scientists inspectors are supposed to interview. Real scientists have been coached by Iraqi officials on what to say. And intelligence sources indicate that Saddam Hussein has ordered that scientists who cooperate with U.N. inspectors in disarming Iraq will be killed, along with their families.

Year after year, Saddam Hussein has gone to elaborate lengths, spent enormous sums, taken great risks, to build and keep weapons of mass destruction—but why? The only possible explanation, the only possible use he could have for those weapons, is to dominate, intimidate, or attack. With nuclear arms or a full arsenal of chemical and biological weapons, Saddam Hussein could resume his ambitions of conquest in the Middle East and create deadly havoc in the region. And this Congress and the American people must recognize another threat. Evidence from intelligence sources, secret communications, and statements by people now in custody reveal that Saddam Hussein aids and protects terrorists, including members of al Qaeda. Secretly, and without fingerprints, he could provide one of his hidden weapons to terrorists, or help them develop their own.

Before September 11, 2001, many in the world believed that Saddam Hussein could be contained. But chemical agents and lethal viruses and shadowy terrorist networks are not easily contained. Imagine those nineteen hijackers with other weapons, and other plans—this time armed by Saddam Hussein. It would take just one vial, one canister, one crate slipped into this country to bring a day of horror like none we have ever known. We will do everything in our power to make sure that day never comes.

Some have said we must not act until the threat is imminent. Since when have terrorists and tyrants announced their intentions, politely putting us on notice before they strike? If this threat is permitted to fully and suddenly emerge, all actions, all words, and all recriminations would come too late. Trusting in the sanity and restraint of Saddam Hussein is not a strategy, and it is not an option.

This dictator, who is assembling the world's most dangerous weapons, has already used them on whole villages—leaving thousands of his own citizens dead, blind, or disfigured. Iraqi refugees tell us how forced confessions are obtained—by torturing children while their parents are made to watch. International human rights groups have catalogued other methods used in the torture chambers of Iraq: electric shock, burning with hot irons, dripping acid on the skin, mutilation with electric drills, cutting out tongues, and rape.

If this is not evil, then evil has no meaning. And tonight I have a message for the brave and oppressed people of Iraq: Your enemy is not surrounding your country—your enemy is ruling your country. And the day he and his regime are removed from power will be the day of your liberation.

The world has waited twelve years for Iraq to disarm. America will not accept a serious and mounting threat to our country, our friends, and our allies. The United States will ask the U.N. Security Council to convene on February 5th to consider the facts of Iraq's ongoing defiance of the world. Secretary of State Powell will present information and intelligence about Iraq's illegal weapons programs; its attempts to hide those weapons from inspectors; and its links to terrorist groups. We will consult, but let there be no misunderstanding: If Saddam Hussein does not fully disarm, for the safety of our people, and for the peace of the world, we will lead a coalition to disarm him.

Tonight I also have a message for the men and women who will keep the peace, members of the American armed forces: Many of you are assembling in and near the Middle East, and some crucial hours may lie ahead. In those hours, the success of our cause will depend on you. Your training has prepared you. Your honor will guide you. You believe in America, and America believes in you.

Sending Americans into battle is the most profound decision a president can make. The technologies of war have changed. The risks and suffering of war have not. For the brave Americans who bear the risk, no victory is free from sorrow. This nation fights reluctantly, because we know the cost, and we dread the days of mourning that always come.

We seek peace. We strive for peace. And sometimes peace must be defended. A future lived at the mercy of terrible threats is no peace at all. If war is forced upon us, we will fight in a just cause and by just means—sparing, in every way we can, the innocent. And if war is forced upon us, we will fight with the full force and might of the United States military—and we will prevail. And as we and our coalition partners are doing in Afghanistan, we will bring to the Iraqi people food and medicines and supplies—and freedom.

Many challenges, abroad and at home, have arrived in a single season. In two years, America has gone from a sense of invulnerability to an awareness of peril, from bitter division in small matters to calm unity in great causes. And we go forward with confidence, because this call of history has come to the right country.

Americans are a resolute people who have risen to every test of our time. Adversity has revealed the character of our country, to the world, and to ourselves.

America is a strong nation, and honorable in the use of our strength. We exercise power without conquest, and sacrifice for the liberty of strangers.

Americans are a free people, who know that freedom is the right of every person and the future of every nation. The liberty we prize is not America's gift to the world, it is God's gift to humanity.

We Americans have faith in ourselves—but not in ourselves alone. We do not claim to know all the ways of Providence, yet we can trust in them, placing our confidence in the loving God behind all of life, and all of history.

May He guide us now, and may God continue to bless the United States of America.

Thank you.

On Saddam Hussein and Iraq

"Some have argued we should wait, and that's an option. In my view, it's the riskiest of all options, because the longer we wait, the stronger and bolder Saddam Hussein will become."

—Cincinnati, Ohio, October 7, 2002

"The triumph of democracy and tolerance in Iraq, in Afghanistan, and beyond would be a grave setback for international terrorism. The terrorists thrive on the support of tyrants and the resentments of oppressed peoples. When tyrants fall, and resentment gives way to hope, men and women in every culture reject the ideologies of terror and turn to the pursuits of peace. Everywhere that freedom takes hold, terror will retreat."

—Address to the nation, September 7, 2003

"After all, this is a guy that tried to kill my dad at one time."

—Houston, Texas, September 26, 2002

"And in 1995, after four years of deception, Iraq finally admitted it had a crash nuclear weapons program prior to the Gulf War. We know now, were it not for that war, the regime in Iraq would likely have possessed a nuclear weapon no later than 1993. Today, Iraq continues to withhold important information about its nuclear program—weapons design, procurement logs, experiment data, an accounting of nuclear materials, and documentation of foreign assistance. Iraq employs capable nuclear scientists and technicians. It retains physical infrastructure needed to build a nuclear weapon. Iraq has made several attempts to buy high-strength aluminum tubes used to enrich uranium for a nuclear weapon. Should Iraq acquire fissile material, it would be able to build a nuclear weapon within a year. And Iraq's state-controlled media has reported numerous meetings between Saddam Hussein and his nuclear scientists, leaving little doubt about his continued appetite for these weapons."

—ADDRESS TO THE UNITED NATIONS,
SEPTEMBER 12, 2002

"And if Iraq regimes continues to defy us, and the world, we will move deliberately, yet decisively, to hold Iraq to account."

—DAVENPORT, IOWA, SEPTEMBER 16, 2002

"[Saddam Hussein] really doesn't care about the opinion of mankind."

—FORT HOOD, TEXAS, JANUARY 3, 2003

"When Iraq is liberated, you [Saddam Hussein] will be treated, tried, and persecuted as a war criminal."

—WASHINGTON, D.C., JANUARY 22, 2003

"[Our enemies] know that a free Iraq will be free of them—free of assassins, and torturers, and secret police. They know that as democracy rises in Iraq, all of their hateful ambitions will fall like the statues of the former dictator. And that is why, five months after we liberated Iraq, a collection of killers is desperately trying to undermine Iraq's progress and throw the country into chaos. Some of the attackers are members of the old Saddam regime, who fled the battlefield and now fight in the shadows. Some of the attackers are foreign terrorists, who have come to Iraq to pursue their war on America and other free nations. We cannot be certain to what extent these groups work together. We do know they have a common goal—reclaiming Iraq for tyranny."

—FROM HIS ADDRESS TO THE NATION ON SEPTEMBER 7, 2003

"The facts are, this is a man who gassed his own people, has invaded two countries, a person who stiffed the international organization time and time again."

—LOUISVILLE, KENTUCKY, SEPTEMBER 5, 2002

"I will first remind the United Nations that for eleven long years, Saddam Hussein has sidestepped, crawfished, wheedled out of any agreement he had made not to harbor—not to develop weapons of mass destruction, agreements he's made to treat the people within his country with respect. And so I'm going to call upon the world to recognize that he is stiffing the world."

—THE WHITE HOUSE, SEPTEMBER 4, 2002

"[Saddam Hussein] is adept at deception and delays and denying. He asked for more time so he can give the so-called inspectors more runaround."

—ST. LOUIS, MISSOURI, JANUARY 22, 2003

"Our strategy in Iraq has three objectives: destroying the terrorists, enlisting the support of other nations for a free Iraq, and helping Iraqis assume responsibility for their own defense and their own future."

— WASHINGTON, D.C., SEPTEMBER 7, 2003

"This violence is directed not only against our coalition, but against anyone in Iraq who stands for decency and freedom and progress. There is more at work in these attacks than blind rage. The terrorists have a strategic goal. They want us to leave Iraq before our work is done. They want to shake the will of the civilized world."

— ON THE LOCALIZED ATTACKS AROUND IRAQ
AGAINST AMERICAN AND BRITISH SOLDIERS
IN THE WEEKS LEADING UP TO HIS ADDRESS
TO THE NATION ON SEPTEMBER 7, 2003

"[Uday and Qusay Hussein were] two of the regime's chief henchmen . . . responsible for torture, maiming and murder of countless Iraqis. Now more than ever all Iraqis can know that the former regime is gone and will not be coming back."

— ROSE GARDEN REMARKS ON THE DEATHS OF
SADDAM HUSSEIN'S SONS, JULY 23, 2003

"The regime must allow immediate and unrestricted access to every site, every document, and every person identified by inspectors. Iraq can be certain that the old game of cheat-and-retreat tolerated at other times will no longer be tolerated."

— WEEKLY RADIO ADDRESS, NOVEMBER 9, 2002

"Nothing he [Saddam Hussein] has done has convinced me . . . that he is the kind of fellow that is willing to forgo weapons of mass destruction . . . to be a peaceful neighbor. . . . He hasn't convinced me, nor has he convinced my administration."

—CRAWFORD, TEXAS, AUGUST 21, 2002

On Peace

"The goals for this country are peace in the world. And the goals for this country are a compassionate America for every single citizen. That compassion is found in the hearts and souls of the American citizens."

—WASHINGTON, D.C., DECEMBER 19, 2002

"I am determined to keep . . . on the road to peace."

—WASHINGTON, D.C., JUNE 10, 2003

"I see a peaceful world, I do. The rest of the world watches us very carefully. I like to say, 'If the United States blinks, they'll go to sleep.' We're not going to blink."

—AT A REPUBLICAN PARTY LUNCHEON, DALLAS, TEXAS, MARCH 29, 2002

"I want you to tell your children that when they hear all the talk and all the speculation and all the thousands of hours of so-called experts babbling away about this, that, or the other, that the true policy of this government is to achieve peace for generations to come."

— SOUTH BEND, INDIANA, SEPTEMBER 5, 2002

"He's had some chance to grab the peace and hasn't done so in the past, and, therefore, he has let down the Palestinian people."

— ON YASSER ARAFAT, WASHINGTON, D.C., MAY 4, 2002

"You need to tell your loved ones, the little ones in particular, that when they hear the president talking about al Qaeda, Iraq, and other places, I do so because I long for peace."

— LOUISVILLE, KENTUCKY, SEPTEMBER 5, 2002

"I assured the prime minister, my administration will . . . work with our nations in the Middle East, [to] give peace a chance. Secondly, I told him that our nation will . . . facilitate peace and that we will work with those responsible for peace."

— DURING A PHOTO OPPORTUNITY WITH ISRAELI PRIME MINISTER
ARIEL SHARON, WASHINGTON, D.C., MARCH 20, 2001

"I believe we can achieve peace at home and I believe we can achieve peace abroad."

— WASHINGTON, D.C., JANUARY 30, 2003

"I appreciate all the members of Congress working to come up with a resolution. It sends a clear signal to the world that this country is determined to disarm Iraq and thereby bring peace to the world."

— WASHINGTON, D.C., OCTOBER 1, 2002

"I believe by being strong, diligent, by speaking out against right from wrong, by calling evil what it is, we can lead the world to a more peaceful tomorrow."

—DES MOINES, IOWA, JUNE 7, 2002

"Listen, I recognize there's going to be extremes, particularly in the Palestinian territories, [who] want to blow up peace."

—WASHINGTON, D.C., JUNE 9, 2003

"It is awfully hard to realize there can be peace in a place like the Middle East."

—GEORGIA INSTITUTE OF TECHNOLOGY,
ATLANTA, GEORGIA, MARCH 27, 2002

His Address to the Nation

SEPTEMBER 7, 2003

G ood evening. I have asked for this time to keep you informed of America's actions in the war on terror. Nearly two years ago, following deadly attacks on our country, we began a systematic campaign against terrorism. These months have been a time of new responsibilities, and sacrifice, and national resolve, and great progress.

America and a broad coalition acted first in Afghanistan, by destroying the training camps of terror and removing the regime that harbored al Qaeda. In a series of raids and actions around the world, nearly two-thirds of al Qaeda's known leaders have been captured or killed, and we continue on al Qaeda's trail. We have exposed terrorist front groups, seized terrorist accounts, taken new measures to protect our homeland, and uncovered sleeper cells inside the United States. And we acted in Iraq, where the former regime sponsored terror, possessed and used weapons of mass destruction, and for twelve years defied the clear demands of the United Nations Security Council. Our coalition enforced these international demands in one of the swiftest and most humane military campaigns in history.

For a generation leading up to September the 11th, 2001, terrorists and their radical allies attacked innocent people in the Middle East and beyond, without facing a sustained and serious response. The terrorists became convinced that free nations were decadent and weak. And they grew bolder, believing that history was on their side. Since America put out the fires of September the 11th, and mourned our dead, and went to war, history has taken a different turn. We have carried the fight to the enemy. We are rolling back the terrorist threat to civilization, not on the fringes of its influence, but at the heart of its power.

This work continues. In Iraq, we are helping the long-suffering people of that country to build a decent and democratic society at the center of the Middle East. Together we are transforming a place of torture chambers and mass graves into a nation of laws and free institutions. This undertaking is difficult and costly—yet worthy of our country and critical to our security.

The Middle East will either become a place of progress and peace, or it will be an exporter of violence and terror that takes more lives in America and in other free nations. The triumph of democracy and tolerance in Iraq, in Afghanistan, and beyond would be a grave setback for international terrorism. The terrorists thrive on the support of tyrants and the resentments of oppressed peoples. When tyrants fall, and resentment gives way to hope, men and women in every culture reject the ideologies of terror and turn to the pursuits of peace. Everywhere that freedom takes hold, terror will retreat.

Our enemies understand this. They know that a free Iraq will be free of them—free of assassins and torturers and secret police. They know that as democracy rises in Iraq, all of their hateful ambitions will fall like the statues of the former dictator. And that is why, five months after we liberated Iraq, a collection of killers is desperately trying to undermine Iraq's progress and throw the country into chaos.

Some of the attackers are members of the old Saddam regime, who fled the battlefield and now fight in the shadows. Some of the attackers are foreign terrorists, who have come to Iraq to pursue their war on America and other free nations. We cannot be certain to what extent these groups work together. We do know they have a common goal—reclaiming Iraq for tyranny.

Most, but not all, of these killers operate in one area of the country. The attacks you have heard and read about in the last few weeks have occurred predominantly in the central region of Iraq, between Baghdad and Tikrit—Saddam Hussein's former stronghold. The north of Iraq is generally stable and is moving forward with reconstruction and self-government. The same trends are evident in the south, despite recent attacks by terrorist groups.

Though their attacks are localized, the terrorists and Saddam loyalists have done great harm. They have ambushed American and British service members—who stand for freedom and order. They have killed civilian aid workers of the United Nations—who represent the compassion and generosity of the world. They have bombed the Jordanian embassy—the symbol of a peaceful Arab country. And last week they murdered a respected cleric and over a hundred Muslims at prayer—bombing a holy shrine and a symbol of Islam's peaceful teachings.

This violence is directed not only against our coalition, but against anyone in Iraq who stands for decency and freedom and progress.

There is more at work in these attacks than blind rage. The terrorists have a strategic goal. They want us to leave Iraq before our work is done. They want to shake the will of the civilized world. In the past, the terrorists have cited the examples of Beirut and Somalia, claiming that if you inflict harm on Americans, we will run from a challenge. In this, they are mistaken.

Two years ago, I told the Congress and the country that the war on terror would be a lengthy war, a different kind of war, fought on many fronts in many places. Iraq is now the central front. Enemies of freedom are making a desperate stand there—and there they must be defeated. This will take time and require sacrifice. Yet we will do what is necessary, we will spend what is necessary, to achieve this essential victory in the war on terror, to promote freedom and to make our own nation more secure.

America has done this kind of work before. Following World War II, we lifted up the defeated nations of Japan and Germany, and stood with them as they built representative governments. We committed years and resources to this cause. And that effort has been repaid many times over in three generations of friendship and peace. America today accepts the challenge of helping Iraq in the same spirit—for their sake, and our own.

Our strategy in Iraq has three objectives: destroying the terrorists, enlisting the support of other nations for a free Iraq, and helping Iraqis assume responsibility for their own defense and their own future.

First, we are taking direct action against the terrorists in the Iraqi theater, which is the surest way to prevent future attacks on coalition forces and the Iraqi people. We are staying on the offensive, with a series of precise strikes against enemy targets increasingly guided by intelligence given to us by Iraqi citizens.

Since the end of major combat operations, we have conducted raids seizing many caches of enemy weapons and massive amounts of ammunition, and we have captured or killed hundreds of Saddam loyalists and terrorists. So far, of the fifty-five most wanted former Iraqi leaders, forty-two are dead or in custody. We are sending a clear message: Anyone who seeks to harm our soldiers can know that our soldiers are hunting for them.

Second, we are committed to expanding international cooperation in the reconstruction and security of Iraq, just as we are in Afghanistan. Our military commanders in Iraq advise me that the current number of American troops—nearly 130,000—is appropriate to their mission. They are joined by over twenty thousand service members from twenty-nine other countries. Two multinational divisions, led by the British and the Poles, are serving alongside our forces—and in order to share the burden more broadly, our commanders have requested a third multinational division to serve in Iraq.

Some countries have requested an explicit authorization of the United Nations Security Council before committing troops to Iraq. I have directed Secretary of State Colin Powell to introduce a new Security Council resolution, which would authorize the creation of a multinational force in Iraq, to be led by America.

I recognize that not all of our friends agreed with our decision to enforce the Security Council resolutions and remove Saddam Hussein from power. Yet we cannot let past differences interfere with present duties. Terrorists in Iraq have attacked representatives of the civilized world, and opposing them must be the cause of the civilized world. Members of the United Nations now have an opportunity—and the responsibility—to assume a broader role in assuring that Iraq becomes a free and democratic nation.

Third, we are encouraging the orderly transfer of sovereignty and authority to the Iraqi people. Our coalition came to Iraq as liberators and we will depart as liberators. Right now Iraq has its own Governing Council, comprised of twenty-five leaders representing Iraq's diverse people. The Governing Council recently appointed cabinet ministers to run government departments. Already more than 90 percent of towns and cities have functioning local governments, which are restoring basic services. We're helping to train civil defense forces to keep order, and an Iraqi police service to enforce the law, a facilities protection service, Iraqi border guards to help secure the borders, and a new Iraqi army. In all these roles, there are now some sixty thousand Iraqi citizens under arms, defending the security of their own country, and we are accelerating the training of more.

Iraq is ready to take the next steps toward self-government. The Security Council resolution we introduce will encourage Iraq's Governing Council to submit a plan and a timetable for the drafting of a constitution and for free elections. From the outset, I have expressed confidence in the ability of the Iraqi people to govern themselves. Now they must rise to the responsibilities of a free people and secure the blessings of their own liberty.

Our strategy in Iraq will require new resources. We have conducted a thorough assessment of our military and reconstruction needs in Iraq, and also in Afghanistan. I will soon submit to Congress a request for $87 billion. The request will cover ongoing military and intelligence operations in Iraq, Afghanistan, and elsewhere, which we expect will cost $66 billion over the next year. This budget request will also support our commitment to helping the Iraqi and Afghan people rebuild their own nations after decades of oppression and mismanagement. We will provide funds to help them improve security. And we will help them to restore basic services, such as electricity and water, and to build new schools, roads, and medical clinics. This effort is essential to the stability of those nations, and, therefore, to our own security. Now and in the future, we will support our troops and we will keep our word to the more than fifty million people of Afghanistan and Iraq.

Later this month, Secretary Powell will meet with representatives of many nations to discuss their financial contributions to the reconstruction of Afghanistan. Next month, he will hold a similar funding conference for the reconstruction of Iraq. Europe, Japan, and states in the Middle East all will benefit from the success of freedom in these two countries, and they should contribute to that success.

The people of Iraq are emerging from a long trial. For them, there will be no going back to the days of the dictator, to the miseries and humiliation he inflicted on that good country. For the Middle East and the world, there will be no going back to the days of fear, when a brutal and aggressive tyrant possessed terrible weapons. And for America, there will be no going back to the era before September the 11th, 2001—to false comfort in a dangerous world. We have learned that terrorist attacks are not caused by the use of strength; they are invited by the perception of weakness. And the surest way to avoid attacks on our own people is to engage the enemy where he lives and plans. We are fighting that enemy in Iraq and Afghanistan today so that we do not meet him again on our own streets, in our own cities.

The heaviest burdens in our war on terror fall, as always, on the men and women of our armed forces and our intelligence services. They have removed gathering threats to America and our friends, and this nation takes great pride in their incredible achievements. We are grateful for their skill and courage, and for their acts of decency, which have shown America's character to the world. We honor the sacrifice of their families. And we mourn every American who has died so bravely, so far from home.

The Americans who assume great risk overseas understand the great cause they are in. Not long ago I received a letter from a captain in the Third Infantry Division in Baghdad. He wrote about his pride in serving a just cause, and about the deep desire of Iraqis for liberty. "I see it," he said, "in the eyes of a hungry people every day here. They are starved for freedom and opportunity." And he concluded, "I just thought you'd like a note from the 'front lines of freedom.'" That Army captain, and all of our men and women serving in the war on terror, are on the front lines of freedom. And I want each of them to know, your country thanks you, and your country supports you.

Fellow citizens: We've been tested these past twenty-four

months, and the dangers have not passed. Yet Americans are responding with courage and confidence. We accept the duties of our generation. We are active and resolute in our own defense. We are serving in freedom's cause—and that is the cause of all mankind.

Thank you, and may God continue to bless America.

On America

"Our nation must come together to unite."

—TAMPA, FLORIDA, JUNE 4, 2001

REPORTER: The NAACP is meeting this week in Houston, as you probably know. And there's been some criticism that you've not attended their convention since the 2000 campaign. How would you respond to that, and respond generally to suggestions from some critics that your civil rights record in the administration is not a stellar one?

PRESIDENT BUSH: Let's see. There I was, sitting around . . . the table with foreign leaders, looking at Colin Powell and Condi Rice.

—THE WHITE HOUSE, JULY 9, 2002

"I can't tell you what it's like to be in Europe, for example, to be talking about the greatness of America. But the true greatness of America are the people."

—UPON VISITING THE JEFFERSON MEMORIAL,
WASHINGTON, D.C., JULY 2, 2001

"I'm thrilled to be here in the bread basket of America because it gives me a chance to remind our fellow citizens that we have an advantage here in America—we can feed ourselves."

— STOCKTON, CALIFORNIA, AUGUST 23, 2002

"The American people is this country's greatest asset."

— ALEXANDRIA, VIRGINIA, FEBRUARY 12, 2003

"We love the fact that people can worship an almighty God any way they see fit here in America."

— PHOENIX, ARIZONA, SEPTEMBER 28, 2002

"And we can show the world the true face of America as well. Oh, it's a diverse face, no question about it, which is our strength, not our weakness. But it's a face that can be bound by common goals and common values. It's a face that can stand squarely in the face of evil by the collective acts of people doing good in America."

— FROM REMARKS AT THE FIRST AFRICAN METHODIST
EPISCOPAL RENAISSANCE CENTER,
LOS ANGELES, CALIFORNIA, APRIL 29, 2002

"But one of the things that rang true yesterday to me, and does every time I make a stop here in America, is that we should never lack confidence in our character, in the character of the American people."

— MILWAUKEE, WISCONSIN, AUGUST 14, 2002

"We've been through a terrorist attack and a national emergency, we've been through a recession, we've been through corporate scandals where CEOs forgot what it means to be a responsible citizen. People didn't tell the truth. They were not responsible to their shareholders and employees. They will be held to account for their irresponsible behavior. And that was a shock to our system. We've been through war."

—ANNANDALE, VIRGINIA, JUNE 17, 2003

"This nation is in the process, I believe, of ushering in a period where . . . each of us are responsible for the decisions we make in life."

—NEW YORK CITY, NEW YORK, FEBRUARY 6, 2002

"I think we're making progress. We understand where the power of this country lays. It lays in the hearts and souls of Americans. . . . It lays in the willingness for people to work hard. But as importantly, it lays in the fact that we've got citizens from all walks of life, all political parties, that are willing to say, I want to love my neighbor. I want to make somebody's life just a little bit better."

—CONCORD MIDDLE SCHOOL,
CONCORD, NORTH CAROLINA, APRIL 11, 2001

"We believe in opportunity for all Americans: Rich and poor, black and white. . . ."

—FROM A SPEECH AT BOB JONES UNIVERSITY,
SOUTH CAROLINA, FEBRUARY 2, 2000

"Whether you're here by birth, or whether you're in America by choice, you contribute to the vitality of our life. And for that, we are grateful."

—WASHINGTON, D.C., MAY 17, 2002

"The true strength of America happens when a neighbor loves a neighbor just like they'd like to be loved themselves."
—ELIZABETH, NEW JERSEY, JUNE 16, 2003

"When it comes to our freedoms—defending our freedoms—and securing our homeland, and protecting our innocent Americans, and never forgetting what happened on September the 11th, we are some kind of tough."
—WASHINGTON, D.C., MAY 14, 2002

"See, we love—we love freedom. That's what they didn't understand. They hate things; we love things. They act out of hatred; we don't seek revenge, we seek justice out of love."
—OKLAHOMA CITY, OKLAHOMA, AUGUST 29, 2002

"It was their determination to stick together and to comfort each other that really defines kind of a new spirit that's prevalent in our country, that when one of us suffer, all of us suffers."
—TO THE MINERS AND THEIR FAMILIES AND RESCUERS
AT THE GREEN TREE FIRE DEPARTMENT
IN A SUBURB WEST OF PITTSBURGH, PENNSYLVANIA,
NEW YORK TIMES, AUGUST 5, 2002

"As I travel our country, I remind our citizens there are thousands of people working as hard as they possibly can to keep America safe."
—PORT ELIZABETH, NEW JERSEY, JUNE 24, 2002

"This is a nation that loves our freedom."
—WASHINGTON, D.C., MAY 17, 2002

"America has never been united by blood or birth or soil. We are bound by ideals that move us beyond our backgrounds, lift us above our interests, and teach us what it means to be citizens. Every child must be taught these principles. Every citizen must uphold them. And every immigrant, by embracing these ideals, makes our country more, not less, American."

—FROM HIS INAUGURAL ADDRESS, JANUARY 20, 2001

"We have a renewed appreciation of the character of America. We are a generous people, a thoughtful people who hurt."

—THOMAS WOOTTEN HIGH SCHOOL,
ROCKVILLE, MARYLAND, OCTOBER 30, 2001

"That's what America is about. . . . We proudly call you an American. We don't say, Show us your birth certificate, how you're born, where you're born."

—SANTA ANA, CALIFORNIA, AUGUST 23, 2002

His Address to
the United Nations

SEPTEMBER 23, 2003

Mr. Secretary General, Mr. President, distinguished delegates, ladies and gentlemen: Twenty-four months ago—and yesterday in the memory of America—the center of New York City became a battlefield, and a graveyard, and the symbol of an unfinished war. Since that day, terrorists have struck in Bali, Mombassa, in Casablanca, in Riyadh, in Jakarta, in Jerusalem—measuring the advance of their cause in the chaos and innocent suffering they leave behind.

Last month, terrorists brought their war to the United Nations itself. The U.N. headquarters in Baghdad stood for order and compassion—and for that reason, the terrorists decided it must be destroyed. Among the twenty-two people who were murdered was Sergio Vieira de Mello. Over the decades, this good and brave man from Brazil gave help to the afflicted in Bangladesh, Cyprus, Mozambique, Lebanon, Cambodia, Central Africa, Kosovo, and East Timor, and was aiding the people of Iraq in their time of need. America joins you, his colleagues, in honoring the memory of Señor Vieira de Mello, and the memory of all who died with him in the service to the United Nations.

By the victims they choose, and by the means they use, the terrorists have clarified the struggle we are in. Those who target relief workers for death have set themselves against all humanity. Those who incite murder and celebrate suicide reveal their contempt for life itself. They have no place in any religious faith; they have no claim on the world's sympathy; and they should have no friend in this chamber.

Events during the past two years have set before us the clearest of divides: between those who seek order and those who spread chaos; between those who work for peaceful change and those who adopt the methods of gangsters; between those who honor the rights of man and those who deliberately take the lives of men and women and children without mercy or shame.

Between these alternatives there is no neutral ground. All governments that support terror are complicit in a war against civilization. No government should ignore the threat of terror, because to look the other way gives terrorists the chance to regroup and recruit and prepare. And all nations that fight terror, as if the lives of their own people depend on it, will earn the favorable judgment of history.

The former regimes of Afghanistan and Iraq knew these alternatives, and made their choices. The Taliban was a sponsor and servant of terrorism. When confronted, that regime chose defiance, and that regime is no more. Afghanistan's president, who is here today, now represents a free people who are building a decent and just society; they're building a nation fully joined in the war against terror.

The regime of Saddam Hussein cultivated ties to terror while it built weapons of mass destruction. It used those weapons in acts of mass murder and refused to account for them when confronted by the world. The Security Council was right to be alarmed. The Security Council was right to demand that Iraq destroy its illegal weapons and prove that it had done so. The Security Council was right to vow serious consequences if Iraq refused to comply. And because there were consequences, because a coalition of nations acted to defend the peace and the credibility of the United Nations, Iraq is free, and today we are joined by representatives of a liberated country.

Saddam Hussein's monuments have been removed and not only his statues. The true monuments of his rule and his character—the torture chambers and the rape rooms and the prison cells for innocent children—are closed. And as we discover the killing fields and mass graves of Iraq, the true scale of Saddam's cruelty is being revealed.

The Iraqi people are meeting hardships and challenges, like every nation that has set out on the path of democracy. Yet their future promises lives of dignity and freedom, and that is a world away from the squalid, vicious tyranny they have known. Across Iraq, life is being improved by liberty. Across the Middle East, people are safer because an unstable aggressor has been removed from power. Across the world, nations are more secure because an ally of terror has fallen.

Our actions in Afghanistan and Iraq were supported by many governments, and America is grateful to each one. I also recognize that some of the sovereign nations of this assembly disagreed with our actions. Yet there was, and there remains, unity among us on the fundamental principles and objectives of the United Nations. We are dedicated to the defense of our collective security and to the advance of human rights. These permanent commitments call us to great work in the world, work we must do together. So let us move forward.

First, we must stand with the people of Afghanistan and Iraq as they build free and stable countries. The terrorists and their allies fear and fight this progress above all, because free people embrace hope over resentment and choose peace over violence.

The United Nations has been a friend of the Afghan people, distributing food and medicine, helping refugees return home, advising on a new constitution, and helping to prepare the way for nationwide elections. NATO has taken over the U.N.-mandated security force in Kabul. American and coalition forces continue to track and defeat al Qaeda terrorists and remnants of the Taliban. Our efforts to rebuild that country go on. I have recently proposed to spend an additional $1.2 billion for the Afghan reconstruction effort, and I urge other nations to continue contributing to this important cause.

In the nation of Iraq, the United Nations is carrying out vital and effective work every day. By the end of 2004, more than 90 percent of Iraqi children under age five will have been immunized against preventable diseases such as polio, tuberculosis and measles, thanks to the hard work and high ideals of UNICEF. Iraq's food distribution system is operational, delivering nearly a half million tons of food per month, thanks to the skill and expertise of the World Food Program.

Our international coalition in Iraq is meeting its responsibilities. We are conducting precision raids against terrorists and holdouts of the former regime. These killers are at war with the Iraqi people. They have made Iraq the central front in the war on terror, and they will be defeated. Our coalition has made sure that Iraq's former dictator will never again use weapons of mass destruction. We are interviewing Iraqi citizens and analyzing records of the old regime to reveal the full extent of its weapons programs and its long campaign of deception. We're training Iraqi police and border guards and a new army so the Iraqi people can assume full responsibility for their own security.

And at the same time, our coalition is helping to improve the daily lives of the Iraqi people. The old regime built palaces while letting schools decay, so we are rebuilding more than a thousand schools. The old regime starved hospitals of resources, so we have helped to supply and reopen hospitals across Iraq. The old regime built up armies and weapons, while allowing the nation's infrastructure to crumble, so we are rehabilitating power plants, water and sanitation facilities, bridges, and airports. I proposed to Congress that the United States provide additional funding for our work in Iraq, the greatest financial commitment of its kind since the Marshall Plan. Having helped to liberate Iraq, we will honor our pledges to Iraq, and by helping the Iraqi people build a stable and peaceful country, we will make our own countries more secure.

The primary goal of our coalition in Iraq is self-government for the people of Iraq, reached by orderly and democratic process. This process must unfold according to the needs of Iraqis, neither hurried nor delayed by the wishes of other parties. And the United Nations can contribute greatly to the cause of Iraq self-government. America is working with friends and allies on a new Security Council resolution, which will expand the U.N.'s role in Iraq. As in the aftermath of other conflicts, the United Nations should assist in developing a constitution, in training civil servants, and conducting free and fair elections.

Iraq now has a Governing Council, the first truly representative institution in that country. Iraq's new leaders are showing the openness and tolerance that democracy requires, and they're also showing courage. Yet every young democracy needs the help of friends. Now the nation of Iraq needs and deserves our aid, and all nations of goodwill should step forward and provide that support.

The success of a free Iraq will be watched and noted throughout the region. Millions will see that freedom, equality, and material progress are possible at the heart of the Middle East. Leaders in the region will face the clearest evidence that free institutions and open societies are the only path to long-term national success and dignity. And a transformed Middle East would benefit the entire world, by undermining the ideologies that export violence to other lands.

Iraq as a dictatorship had great power to destabilize the Middle East; Iraq as a democracy will have great power to inspire the Middle East. The advance of democratic institutions in Iraq is setting an example that others, including the Palestinian people, would be wise to follow. The Palestinian cause is betrayed by leaders who cling to power by feeding old hatreds and destroying the good work of others. The Palestinian people deserve their own state, and they will gain that state by embracing new leaders committed to reform, to fighting terror, and to building peace. All parties in the Middle East must meet their responsibilities and carry out the commitments they made at Aqaba. Israel must work to create the conditions that will allow a peaceful Palestinian state to emerge. And Arab nations must cut off funding and other support for terrorist organizations. America will work with every nation in the region that acts boldly for the sake of peace.

A second challenge we must confront together is the proliferation of weapons of mass destruction. Outlaw regimes that possess nuclear, chemical, and biological weapons—and the means to deliver them—would be able to use blackmail and create chaos in entire regions. These weapons could be used by terrorists to bring sudden disaster and suffering on a scale we can scarcely imagine. The deadly combination of outlaw regimes and terror networks and weapons of mass murder is a peril that cannot be ignored or wished away. If such a danger is allowed to fully materialize, all words, all protests, will come too late. Nations of the world must have the wisdom and the will to stop grave threats before they arrive.

One crucial step is to secure the most dangerous materials at their source. For more than a decade, the United States has worked with Russia and other states of the former Soviet Union to dismantle, destroy, or secure weapons and dangerous materials left over from another era. Last year in Canada, the G8 nations agreed to provide up to $20 billion—half of it from the United States—to fight this proliferation risk over the next ten years. Since then, six additional countries have joined the effort. More are needed, and I urge other nations to help us meet this danger.

We're also improving our capability to interdict lethal materials in transit. Through our Proliferation Security Initiative, eleven nations are preparing to search planes and ships, trains and trucks carrying suspect cargo, and to seize weapons or missile shipments that raise proliferation concerns. These nations have agreed on a set of interdiction principles, consistent with current legal authorities. And we're working to expand the Proliferation Security Initiative to other countries. We're determined to keep the world's most destructive weapons away from all our shores, and out of the hands of our common enemies.

Because proliferators will use any route or channel that is open to them, we need the broadest possible cooperation to stop them. Today, I ask the U.N. Security Council to adopt a new anti-proliferation resolution. This resolution should call on all members of the U.N. to criminalize the proliferation of weapons—weapons of mass destruction, to enact strict export controls consistent with international standards, and to secure any and all sensitive materials within their own borders. The United States stands ready to help any nation draft these new laws and to assist in their enforcement.

A third challenge we share is a challenge to our conscience. We must act decisively to meet the humanitarian crises of our time. The United States has begun to carry out the Emergency Plan for AIDS Relief, aimed at preventing AIDS on a massive scale and treating millions who have the disease already. We have pledged $15 billion over five years to fight AIDS around the world.

My country is acting to save lives from famine, as well. We're providing more than $1.4 billion in global emergency food aid, and I've asked our United States Congress for $200 million for a new famine fund, so we can act quickly when the first signs of famine appear. Every nation on every continent should generously add their resources to the fight against disease and desperate hunger.

There's another humanitarian crisis spreading, yet hidden from view. Each year, an estimated 800,000 to 900,000 human beings are bought, sold, or forced across the world's borders. Among them are hundreds of thousands of teenage girls, and others as young as five, who fall victim to the sex trade. This commerce in human life generates billions of dollars each year—much of which is used to finance organized crime.

There's a special evil in the abuse and exploitation of the most innocent and vulnerable. The victims of sex trade see little of life before they see the very worst of life—an underground of brutality and lonely fear. Those who create these victims and profit from their suffering must be severely punished. Those who patronize this industry debase themselves and deepen the misery of others. And governments that tolerate this trade are tolerating a form of slavery.

This problem has appeared in my own country, and we are working to stop it. The PROTECT Act, which I signed into law this year, makes it a crime for any person to enter the United States, or for any citizen to travel abroad, for the purpose of sex tourism involving children. The Department of Justice is actively investigating sex tour operators and patrons, who can face up to thirty years in prison. Under the Trafficking Victims Protection Act, the United States is using sanctions against governments to discourage human trafficking.

The victims of this industry also need help from members of the United Nations. And this begins with clear standards and the certainty of punishment under laws of every country. Today, some nations make it a crime to sexually abuse children abroad. Such conduct should be a crime in all nations. Governments should inform travelers of the harm this industry does, and the severe punishments that will fall on its patrons. The American government is committing $50 million to support the good work of organizations that are rescuing women and children from exploitation, and giving them shelter and medical treatment and the hope of a new life. I urge other governments to do their part.

We must show new energy in fighting back an old evil. Nearly two centuries after the abolition of the transatlantic slave trade, and more than a century after slavery was officially ended in its last strongholds, the trade in human beings for any purpose must not be allowed to thrive in our time.

All the challenges I have spoken of this morning require urgent attention and moral clarity. Helping Afghanistan and Iraq to succeed as free nations in a transformed region, cutting off the avenues of proliferation, abolishing modern forms of slavery—these are the kinds of great tasks for which the United Nations was founded. In each case, careful discussion is needed, and also decisive action. Our good intentions will be credited only if we achieve good outcomes.

As an original signer of the U.N. Charter, the United States of America is committed to the United Nations. And we show that commitment by working to fulfill the U.N.'s stated purposes and give meaning to its ideals. The founding documents of the United Nations and the founding documents of America stand in the same tradition. Both assert that human beings should never be reduced to objects of power or commerce, because their dignity is inherent. Both require—both recognize a moral law that stands above men and nations, which must be defended and enforced by men and nations. And both point the way to peace, the peace that comes when all are free. We secure that peace with our courage, and we must show that courage together.

May God bless you all.

On Faith and Religion

"Faith . . . teaches us not merely to tolerate one another, but to respect one another—to show a regard for different views and the courtesy to listen. This is essential to democracy."

—From a speech at a national prayer breakfast, February 6, 2001

"I couldn't imagine somebody like Osama bin Laden understanding the joy of Hanukkah."

—The White House, December 10, 2001

"I don't think that witchcraft is a religion. I wish the military would rethink this decision."

—On Fort Hood's decision to allow Wiccan rituals, to ABC News, June 1999

"The course of this conflict is not known, yet its outcome is certain. Freedom and fear, justice and cruelty, have always been at war, and we know that God is not neutral between them."

—Address to Joint Session of Congress, September 20, 2001

"Our priority is our faith."

— DAYTON, OHIO, JULY 31, 2000

"See, they've hijacked a great religion, and they don't care about life. They've got their desires, their dark, dark ambitions. And if people get in the way from them, that's just too bad, as far as they're concerned."

— SOUTH BEND, INDIANA, SEPTEMBER 5, 2002

"My faith tells me that acceptance of Jesus Christ as my savior is my salvation, and I believe I made it clear that it is not the governor's role to decide who goes to heaven. I believe God decides who goes to heaven, not George W. Bush."

— ACCORDING TO THE *HOUSTON CHRONICLE*
WHEN HE WAS THE GOVERNOR
OF TEXAS IN 1998

"Faith crosses every border and touches every heart in every nation."

— NATIONAL PRAYER BREAKFAST,
WASHINGTON, D.C., FEBRUARY 16, 2001

"We can also be confident in the ways of Providence, even when they are far from our understanding. Events aren't moved by blind change and chance. Behind all of life and all of history, there's a dedication and purpose, set by the hand of a just and faithful God. And that hope will never be shaken."

— WASHINGTON, D.C., FEBRUARY 6, 2003

"One of the great things about this country is a lot of people pray."

—WASHINGTON, D.C., APRIL 13, 2003

"There is a role for government. When we fund programs, we ought not to discriminate against faith-based programs. And we ought not to cause the faith-based program to have to change its mission in order to receive any money. Otherwise it won't be a faith-based program. It will fall into the old government program."

—LOS ANGELES, CALIFORNIA, APRIL 29, 2002

"They can't stand religion."

—ON THE ISLAMIC EXTREMISTS THOUGHT TO BE TERRORISTS,
ST. PETERSBURG UNIVERSITY,
ST. PETERSBURG, RUSSIA, MAY 25, 2002

"I cannot speak strongly enough about how we must collectively get after those who kill in the name of . . . some kind of false religion."

—AT A PRESS CONFERENCE WITH KING ABDULLAH
OF JORDAN, AUGUST 1, 2002

"We believe in freedom. We believe freedom is universal. We believe freedom is a gift from the Almighty God for every person, regardless of their race or their religion."

—BETHESDA, MARYLAND, APRIL 11, 2003

"But one way is for religion to be introduced—is for me—you know, my heart was changed—one heart at a time, my little old heart."

—*U.S. NEWS & WORLD REPORT*, DECEMBER 6, 1999

"I don't believe God picked who was going to be the president."
— FROM AN INTERVIEW WITH BARBARA WALTERS,
DECEMBER 4, 2001

On Himself

"I'm the master of low expectations."

—ABOARD *AIR FORCE ONE*, JUNE 4, 2003

"I'm a patient man, which is hard for me to believe."

—*SAN FRANCISCO CHRONICLE*, FEBRUARY 25, 2000

"I've described myself as a compassionate conservative, because I am convinced a conservative philosophy is a compassionate philosophy that frees individuals to achieve their highest potential. It is conservative to cut taxes and compassionate to give people more money to spend. It is conservative to insist upon local control of schools and high standards and results; it is compassionate to make sure every child learns to read and no one is left behind. It is conservative to reform the welfare system by insisting on work; it's compassionate to free people from dependency on government. It is conservative to reform the juvenile justice code to insist on consequences for bad behavior;

it is compassionate to recognize that discipline and love go hand in hand."

—From his speech announcing his consideration of the Republican nomination for the presidency of the United States, March 7, 1999

"As I understand it, the current FBI form asks the question, 'Did somebody use drugs within the last seven years?' and I will be glad to answer that question, and the answer is no."

—*Time* magazine, August 18, 2000

"And there will be—I take it back. It will be a signature—I won't hesitate. It will probably take about—you know, about three seconds to get to the W, I may hesitate on the period, and then rip through the Bush."

—On how he creates his signature, Washington, D.C., March 24, 2002

"I try to go for longer runs, but it's tough around here at the White House on the outdoor track. It's sad that I can't run longer. It's one of the saddest things about the presidency."

—*Washington Post*, August 21, 2002

"Home is important. It's important to have a home."

—Crawford, Texas, February 18, 2001

"I can assure you, when I was a senior in high school, I never sat in an audience saying, Gosh, if I work hard, I'll be president of the United States."

—Crawford High School, Crawford, Texas, November 15, 2001

"Let me put it to you this way, I am not a revengeful person."
— FROM AN INTERVIEW WITH *TIME* MAGAZINE,
DECEMBER 25, 2000

"I'm a patient man, and so is the American people . . . much to the chagrin of the enemy that still wants to take us on."
— BRIDGEPORT, CONNECTICUT, APRIL 9, 2002

"One of the interesting things to do is drink coffee and watch [the dog] Barney chase armadillos. The armadillos are out, and they love to root in our flower bed. It's good that Barney routs them out of their rooting."
— DESCRIBING HIS TEXAS RANCH LIFE TO
USA TODAY REPORTER JUDY KEEN, AUGUST 22, 2001

"I'm a uniter, not a divider. That means when it comes time to sew up your chest cavity, we use stitches as opposed to opening it up."
— *LATE SHOW WITH DAVID LETTERMAN*, MARCH 2, 2000

"I come from a different generation from my dad. And I think my experiences have enriched me as a person and prepared me for the leadership role. . . ."
— *THE NEWSHOUR WITH JIM LEHRER*, APRIL 27, 2000